Christian Perspectives on Sex and Marriage

WILLIAM FITCH

"It is not good for man to be alone."

WILLIAM B. EERDMANS PUBLISHING COMPANY
Grand Rapids, Michigan

Library of Congress Catalog Card Number: 78-168436
Printed in the United States of America

Foreword

Apart from the fact that a reasonable and comprehensive understanding of human sexual behavior and its many nuances might be considered a basic human (and humane) right, do we really need yet another book expounding this topic? I believe we do, and furthermore, I feel we must have this subject presented for the Christian against a backdrop of Christian principles. "Backdrop" is hardly the proper word; better one should say we need this subject permeated with Christian principle and applicable in our daily life as an integral part of our Christian witness.

For almost two thousand years the Christian church has been involved in the field of education. She has had to divorce herself from many of these educational responsibilities as fields of knowledge expanded and facilities fell short of the needs of the people. Today, one of the strongholds of the Christian church—the family unit—is threatened by mass disruption, if not extinction, and the Christian principles behind the family unit must be forcefully expounded and firmly upheld. Basic to this is an honest and complete family life program where modern mores are debated, normal and abnormal sexual patterns are discussed, and scripturally based Christian views concerning sexual matters are presented openly and honestly.

In the past, most Christians have broached the topic of sexual habits, patterns, and problems—if at all—with some fear and trepidation, usually with limited depth of understanding, and often with much bias based on personal experience. One is not too surprised that this was so if the grounding was inadequate, incomplete, and often inconsistent. It has been said that we all must learn to add and subtract before we learn to multiply—speaking arithmetically. Need we say more concerning limited sex education?

But now, this need no longer be the case, for we have between these covers a unique handbook on Christian attitudes towards sex and marriage presented in a friendly, almost matter-of-fact manner that immediately should put one at ease. That in itself is no small accomplishment when dealing with this subject. Needless to say, if one cannot be at ease in his reading of such vital personal issues, then can he anticipate in his pattern of functioning anything short of *dis*-ease, be it psychological, social, physical, or emotional?

Almost characteristic of the generations of Christians before us has been the manner in which they have superficially glossed over, if not adroitly avoided, this delicate topic. In some instances there has been almost a resistance to the fact that sex even existed! But it did then, it does now, and it will continue to do so. Our understanding of its fullest purpose, along with our attitude towards our own sexual potential, should be guided by the light of scriptural truths and based on biblical principles. Dr. Fitch has done this for us in a style that lends itself well to individual perusal, group presentation, or family discussion. From a wealth of experience in individual counselling in this field, and supported by a sound theological background and biblical foundation, Dr. Fitch writes. I know he does so out of a sense of deep personal concern that these matters are of great importance for the fullest Christian experience possible.

—John R. Taylor, M.D., F.R.C.S. (C)
Women's College Hospital
Toronto, Canada

Contents

Acknowledgments

I am deeply indebted to the many people who have made the writing of this book possible.

First and foremost, of course, are the countless couples who through the years have shared with me the problems they have faced and have permitted me to share with them in what is a very sacred area of life.

Then, too, I have had incalculable help from several members of the medical profession. Dr. John MacKenzie of the Workmen's Compensation Hospital in Toronto has been a true sounding board for many of my ideas. Dr. John Taylor, Gynecologist and Obstetrician of the Women's College Hospital, Toronto, has read the manuscript more than once and has given some excellent advice. Mr. Stan Skarsten, for several years recently Psychologist in Chief at the Clarke Institute of Mental Health and Leader of the Christian Marriage Counselling Bureau in Toronto, has also provided many leads which he will readily recognize in this book.

My own wife has been my teacher and mentor for many years in things that concern the woman's mind. Without her help this book could not have been written.

To them all I say, Thank you, and that very sincerely.

1: Introduction

In a study group in church recently one young man suggested that most young people arrive at the facts of sex on a trial and error basis.

He is probably right. Even in our modern, permissive Seventies, there are very few places to which young people can go and get the right kind of information. Yet, it is absolutely essential that they find the truth about sex and marriage on the very highest of levels and there is no reason why this should not be. I write this book to help young people to discover the whole truth and nothing but the truth on these all-important matters. I write it also for the sake of many Christian parents who are baffled in their attempts to communicate with their children in areas so sensitive and delicate. It is the birthright of the youth of our churches that they should know the full truth in this vital area of their lives. We fail them if we hold anything back.

It has been my privilege to share in the marriage of thousands of young people. I am not exaggerating. I recall once officiating at ten weddings on a Friday; and then fulfilling the same office at nine more the following day. This happened in Scotland. The reason for the rush of weddings was that we had reached the last two days of the government's fiscal year and by being married within that year the young couples could reclaim a whole year's income tax. What Scotsman would ever pass up such an opportunity! In the course of the years I have seen almost every kind of situation. I have asked at the appropriate time if "anyone had any objection to this marriage now proceeding" and have had objection made. I have seen children born, watched them grow, fall in love, and I have finally shared in their wedding. It has been an especial joy to counsel in hundreds of cases and to go over with the bride and groom the kind of questions they were all too eager to ask. It is one of the greatest joys of any Pastor's life to be with such young Christian people and to share the glad hour when they become "heirs together of the grace of life." Without prejudice, I say that there is nothing more wonderful than a Christian wedding. To have some part in helping make the marriage hold fast against all the assaults of modern temptations has also been most rewarding. My hope is that this book will provide insights and understanding which will help a great many more who will in days to come prepare for their wedding day.

One thing I want to say, however, and to say it at once. This book is not a "how-to" book. There are scores of these on the market. *Ideal Marriage,* its physiology and technique, by Th. H. Van De Velde, for example, has gone through at least forty-five editions and is a classic in its field. All you need to know about methodology in sexual intercourse will be found there. But only to mention this book is to recall another score. Over two and a half million copies of John Eichenlaub's book *The Marriage Art* are in print, and there also any couple who want basic helps in how best to adjust themselves to one another in the moment of sexual ecstasy will find much help. This is not my intention. There is no need to duplicate what has already been competently done. What I wish to do is to present sex and marriage within the only context where it is really seen as God's great gift to man—that is, as part of the divine program for unifying and perfecting the marriage bond between husband and wife. Most of the writing on sex in recent times has not been done from a specifically Christian point of view. Believing as I do that sex can only be understood with a Christian context, I write the following pages to make this emphatically clear and to state without prejudice that it is they who know the joy of being joined to Christ who fully know the joy of being joined together within the marriage bond. This then is my intent. The book is rightly called *Christian Perspectives on Sex and Marriage.* This does not mean that it will not have relevance for the non-Christian. On the contrary. Since marriage is so basically bound into God's creation ordinances, it may well be that in reading this text many who have not yet seen the full purposes of God in creation, and the glory He has designed for man in Christ, may be compellingly drawn to the

Son of God, the only Lord and Saviour of all mankind. For this I pray. Towards this end I write as I do.

There are some who never know the happiness of wedlock. This is one of the facts of life that many young people have to face as they reach the thirties and beyond without having found a partner of their choice. What can one say about this? Some very necessary things. First of all, face the fact without self-pity. God makes no mistakes. What is happening is of His dispensation if you are truly His child. Christ spoke of this. He said that there were some who would not know marriage by the accident of birth, or by the will of others, or by their own determination. He did add, however, that there was always some special niche to be filled by the unmarried in His Church. Every minister of the Word and Sacraments knows of people within this category. In many cases there is real heartache and burden. But it is nevertheless true that a great host of ministries are fulfilled within the fellowship of the Church by unmarried women which no one else could fulfill. Whatever God ordains is always right. He makes no mistakes. And if for some reason or other you find yourself reading these pages and yet the joy of marriage has not been granted you, read on. You may find that what is written here will be of surpassing importance to others; and you may be the one that God wants to use to pass the truth along.

At the same time, we should recognize that God's "normal" for man and woman is that they should marry and beget children. "It is not good for man to be alone: I will make an helpmeet for him." This word from the earliest pages of revelation is a word that has never ceased to be effective through every generation. Marriage is a holy state of life, instituted by God and blessed by our Lord Jesus Christ. It was given in order that natural instincts and affections should be fulfilled and perfected and that thus, in holiness and purity of living, mankind should dwell together in families according to the Word of God. It is cause for great alarm when marriage ceases to hold a pre-eminent standard in society. Today a veritable landslide of catastrophic proportions has taken place. Trial marriages, pre-marital sex, common-law living are all too tragically known to all of us. Our movie houses glory in extolling anything that denies the Christian ethic on marriage. Erotic literature creates the impression that everyone is indulging himself in sensual activities. But this is not God's way. Betrothal and engagement are not devices that man has carved out for the security of his life. On the contrary. They are God's gifts to men; gifts that should be received as a sacred trust. Espousal of man and woman to one another is the right approach to marriage. Such a time in one's life is very sacred if you are really prepared to be serious. True love is very demanding; it wants only the best. And true love is very pure. It has no time for profane and base elements. When a young Christian couple enter on this stage of their life, they should get to know one another more intimately, become accustomed to each other's idiosyncrasies and oddities, and begin to live in anticipation of the days when they will truly be one. Monogamy has always been God's standard. Let Him perfect everything that concerns you and the one you love. Let Him guide you in all the details that lead to your wedding day. And after that, see to it that you constantly "commit your way unto the Lord and trust also in Him."

I have tried to make the following pages as informative and straightforward as possible. Remember this. Sex is beautiful. When God gave to man and woman the gift of sex He shared some of His essential nature with them. There is no doubt that we do not fully understand the meaning of being made "in the image of God" if we do not see that sex is right in there at the center of this great mystery. Beauty, creativity, purity and love are the natural expressions of a God who has made "all things lovely in their time." And in the pure espousal of Christian man and maid, the Holy Three are with us, the threefold grace is said. Sex and marriage are God's gifts. See that you use them to His glory.

2: Finding the Right Partner

I have often heard it said that God has a plan for everyone's life. That means, I suppose, that He has really made a choice of a life-partner for me. How do I discover God's will?

Well, of all the questions you may ask me this is certainly the most important. It is certainly a biblical truth that God has a plan for every life. Jesus Christ was very emphatic about this. He said: "I came forth from the Father not to do mine own will, but the will of Him that sent Me" (John 6:38). The same commission that rested on the Master, rests on all His disciples. We are called to do the will of God. This, and nothing less than this, is the high-calling of God—the will of God, nothing more, nothing less, nothing else.

Obviously, then, when the time comes for me to seek for a life-partner, I must do it under His direction. That's where so many go wrong. They fall in love—or think they do—and then they ask God's blessing on what has happened. But they have really put the cart before the horse. The first thing to do is to set yourself to discover what God's plan for you is.

He has said that He will guide you. That is one of the greatest revelations about God in all the Bible. He is a guiding God. When you place yourself in His hands, He undertakes to lead you "in the right way." God is sovereign. That means He knows everything about everything and about everybody; and it also means that He can bring His plans to complete fulfillment. He won't leave you till He has shown you what is best for you. You can therefore with total confidence place all your trust in Him. He already knows the one He wants you to marry. And if you "seek first the kingdom of God and His righteousness" then He will certainly make very plain at the right time the one that He has chosen for you.

The all-important thing is to yield your life to Him. You can never know any of His special blessings in your life till you have met Him face to face, yielded your life to Jesus Christ as Lord and Saviour and taken the Holy Spirit as your instructor and guide. Once you have done this, God begins to show His hand. Step by step He directs. You will know the will of God because He has said you will. You must leave the methods to Him. Details are always important when God is in them. If your life is yielded to God, He will do the rest.

Does this mean that when the time comes for me to look for a life-partner, I do nothing at all?

No! Of course not. You keep yourself busy in Christ's work wherever you are. You have of course committed the matter to God in prayer and you are regularly asking Him to guide you to the one of His choosing. Okay! You get involved in different kinds of work around the church or in some special branch of youth activities. This means that you are thrown into others' company constantly. Friendships are born this way. Then you begin to find yourself drawn to someone specially. You naturally ask yourself: Is this the one of God's choice? It may be. On the other hand, it may not. You keep on working and praying and, if the attachment that has drawn you to one particular person persists and stays with you, if you find that life seems very empty if you can't share the things that you are thinking about with that person, and if increasingly you want to see and to be with that one, then it may be that God is showing you very simply that this is the one.

Is it at this point that you think we should begin to go steady?

Possibly. But you must act wisely here. I know some young people who want to go steady when they're hardly into their teens. That can be very foolish. Equally, you may cut yourself off from many wonderful friendships if you get into the habit of only seeing and talking with one person. This whole idea of going steady with a boy or a girl for a while and meantime neglecting a host of others may well result in your getting what you want but not getting what you need. The whole idea of going steady has been played up in so many wonderful ways that it's very easy to fall into the trap. And trap it is. If you reach a point in your relationship where nothing else matters to you but being together, then you can be sure that the whole relationship is unhealthy.

In any case, at what age do you think a couple should begin to go steady?

I know that it is very natural for you to want to be with young people like yourself, and it is the most natural thing also for you to want at times to be alone with someone of the other sex, but be careful. If you really believe that God has His hand on your life, you can safely await His timing. God is never late. You may think that your parents are quite stupid and that they don't understand your generation. You may feel over and over again that they place restraints on you and that they don't trust you as you think they should. Hold it. Don't be in too big a hurry. The two biggest decisions you will ever make are (1) what will you do with Jesus who is called the Christ? and (2) whom will you marry? Everything else fades into insignificance alongside these questions. Going steady when you hardly know anything at all about life, its demands, its tensions, its joys and heartbreaks, its opportunities and problems, can be rather foolish.

On the whole I think that going steady is not the best road to reach your desired goal. There is great safety in numbers. There is also a tremendous amount of blessing and help, fun and amusement you can share in, if you maintain a perfectly normal attitude to all your friends, and let God gradually convince you of the one of His choice.

What about dating?

Now, there's a much better idea. By dating you mean taking a friend out for a meal, to a concert, or to some special function at school, college or business. Fine! This is great! What an opportunity you have to get to know someone better! You can choose a variety of friends for different occasions, and this is all to the good. In this way, you can widen the circle of your friendships, and this is one of the most important things for a young person to do. Dating is one of the simplest ways of ensuring that you will be in the company of a friend with whom you want to spend an evening together. You can learn much about each other in a very little time.

Most of what I am saying is really addressed to teenagers. But that is natural and inevitable. It is as you move through your middle teens that you are going to be faced with many of your greatest problems; and yet in so many cases you find it difficult to discuss these things with your parents. Very few adolescents receive much knowledge about sex at home even in our so-called enlightened age. There may be good reason for this, because in human beings, unlike other creatures, sexuality usually involves in some degree thoughts of embarrassment and also of guilt. Just because of this very fact, I always try to speak with the greatest frankness when addressing a group of teenagers or older young people on the question of sex. Some of the most thrilling encounters I have had with the young people of my churches have occurred when I discussed this theme, answering questions and leading them on to make explicit what for so long they have wanted to ask.

Dating should be marked by every Christian young person with consideration, caution and candor. You must respect the one you date and pay her or him every atom of esteem and regard that is rightfully due. You are at an age when it is natural for you to be curious and being alone with one of the other sex inevitably stirs sexual and romantic feelings within you. You are not unique in this. You are absolutely normal. The glandular changes of early adolescence are coursing strongly through you, and the time has come when the other sex has a magnetic attraction. Be sure that as and when you go out with your date, you have committed the whole night to God in prayer and that you are counting on His help to make everything lovely, pure and good.

My folks never told me a thing. Sex was taboo at home.

Too bad! Too bad for both the parents and child. For there is no better place to get the right ideas than at home. Of course, there is a sense in which attitude counts for more than words; and if you happen to have been brought up in a home where your father and mother showed tenderness and respect to one another, you have already learned a great deal. Where there is this kind of mutual regard between parents, the children automatically, I believe, grow up expecting this sort of relationship for themselves and look for and give it when the right moment comes. It is good to have the supper table a place where any subject can be openly discussed and where any question can be honestly asked.

It is always an open question as to how much a parent should teach a child. Much depends on circumstances and the personalities involved. But certain things are worth saying, and I include them now just in case they may have slipped past you. For one thing, be very slow to listen to advice on sexual matters given you by other teenagers. There are plenty of wrong ideas and practices that may go by the name of "smart" but in reality they are not so. Check these things out from other sources or with other people. Another thing that I always add is that pornography is for the birds. I know only too well that no one gets to the age you have reached without having seen some glaring examples of pornographic art. Hugh Hefner's *Playboy* is based entirely on this. Keep this at the right distance from you. I don't say you shouldn't read it occasionally and things like it in order to know what the world and its sin are like; but be careful. You won't find there what you really must know if you are to live in such a way as "to glorify God and to enjoy Him forever." You are responsible for what you know. It is vital that you should know the true facts of life and that means all the essential facts about human sexuality.

All right; start learning. This book is meant to help you learn everything that you need to know to make your dating, your mating, your marriage—indeed, all your life and home and family—the pure gems God means them to be.

I can't help thinking that most adult Christians are really hypocrites when it comes to talking or thinking about this whole subject. Don't you feel so too?

Unfortunately I must agree.

In our Western world adults in general show quite contradictory attitudes to sex. Sometimes they talk as though it was utterly sacred; the next moment it couldn't be more profane.

Sometimes they associate it with shame and at other times they make it a theme for ribaldry. There is no doubt that this is so.

And there is no doubt that the same holds true of the Christian Church in general. Instead of speaking of sex as what it really is—something both natural and noble—they push it under the rug. Instead of talking in plain words to the youth of their church they scarcely ever include a course on sex education in any of their Bible school programming. The result is calamitous. Instead of being kept out in the open where the winds of God are strong and free, the subject is hushed up, forbidden, verboten. Part of the reason for this is that sex in our Western world has been treated in an intensely puritanical fashion—and I use the word puritanical advisedly. It has become a bad word. It has lost the original glory of what the Puritans in all their strength and nobility gave to the world. Into this word have come connotations of rigidness, severity, prudery and hypocrisy. Because of an early association with such connotations, the subject of sex has been difficult to discuss, and an adjustment to a much more open attitude has been painful. The result is that many of our young people today think of themselves and of sex and love in terms of pure biology. But this is also begging the question. There is far more to love than molecules and protoplasm. Many of the finest aspects of youth—creativity, idealism, adventuresomeness and sheer joy of living—are products of the capacity to love and be loved. When they try to deny the really spiritual aspects of love they will only get more mixed up; and this can only end in disappointments in dating and later on during years of marriage.

If you don't have a date, you're a real square.

So they say. This is one of the unhealthy and unnatural aspects of modern life. It is another aspect of life in which you simply have to "keep up with the Joneses." Imitation and competition get mixed up with the search for security in social life and the mood amounts almost to frenzy. I recall a girl graduating from Nursing School who couldn't get a date to escort her. I have seldom witnessed such agony in a girl's eyes. She felt literally rejected by society; and in the end she left the city for the period of the festivities. For a Christian, this is a problem that can be "taken to the Lord in prayer." Thank God, He understands our deepest needs, His love never fails, and His wisdom guides us so unerringly. We can trust in Him forever and know that all is well.

How can you be absolutely sure that you have found God's choice?

Well, let's remember what He has promised. He has said: "The meek He will guide with judgment–that is, with wisdom and good understanding–the meek He will teach His way" (Psalm 25:9). Now that is a very emphatic statement. It comes from the pen of Israel's poet-king, and if ever a man was guided David was. He speaks of God's guidance constantly. Psalm 23 is one of divine guidance all the way: "He leadeth me beside the still waters; He leadeth me in the paths of righteousness for His name's sake." It is out of personal experience that David is speaking here. And the God of the Bible didn't die when David died. On the contrary! He is "the same, yesterday and today and forever" (Hebrews 13:8). That means that you and I can know as David did the guidance of God. He has promised this. And God cannot lie.

All right, let's put this to the test. You are in a certain set of circumstances and you don't know what to do. You are certain that there is a right way and a wrong way and it is in the right way you want to know. You know already that everything that is good and holy and sacred and lovely and pure is of God. He will therefore never lead you into any unsanctified or sinful situation. He will never lead you into a mixed-up condition, for "God is not the author of confusion" (I Corinthians 14:33). And He will never lead you into anything but His "good and perfect and acceptable will" (Romans 12:1), if you really want to know His will. Put Him to the test then. Try God. Test Him. I don't mean that you lay down a set of conditions and say: "God, meet these conditions and I'll know you are God and a guiding God." That is not exactly how He works. What He does is this. He gives you first of all a sense that a certain course is right. You pray more about that and the conviction deepens. You possibly have a friend with whom you are in the habit of praying and you ask her or him to share the problem with you. You pray together. As you do, the conviction becomes even more definite that this is what God wants. And at last you realize that all your contradictions are silenced by His Word of peace. So He leads you on.

Let Him lead thee blindfold onwards,
Love needs not to know;
Children whom the Father feedeth,
Ask not where they go.
Though the path be all unknown,
Over moors and mountains lone.

Give no ear to reason's questions;
Let the blind man hold
That the sun is but a fable
Men believed of old.
At the breast the babe will grow;
Whence the milk he need not know.

Now this guidance is supernatural guidance. It has got to be. You must be left in no doubt that you are in the way and being led by the Spirit of God. Well, this assurance He gives. And in this all-important matter of finding the one of God's choice for you, I promise you He will not disappoint you.

I could take the rest of this book telling you how he led me to the one who has for more than thirty years been the companion of my way and sharer of all my ministry. She was teaching missionary school in Peru, but somehow as I prayed about the future and the possibility of marriage, there was only one face that filled the mirror of my mind. Resolutely I tried to put it away. But it would not go. Eventually I wrote her and asked if she would think of marrying me. I waited long for that letter. Millennia seemed to pass as I awaited eagerly the reply. Judge of my heartache when the reply came back saying, "No, the need here is too great and I could not possibly think of leaving!"

Well, the years rolled along—another six of them—and she came home on furlough. We met, not by accident, but by design, for I asked her to come and address a weekend conference of young people. She came. Hesitatingly, and after much soul-searching and prayer, I asked her to be mine. And this time, the answer was "Yes."

Through these years I believe that God was silently planning for us and preparing us, in ways that we little knew, for what lay ahead. To the glory of God I say it. He left me in no doubt as to the one He chose.

How long should an engagement last?

A good and very important question. The time element varies from culture to culture. Generally speaking, however, it is never wise to rush into marriage quickly. Recently I talked with a young man whose wife had left him that very day.

"How long did you know one another before being married?"

"About three months."

"How long were you engaged?"

"Six weeks."

"Wouldn't a longer period of adjustment have been better for you both?"

"Of course it would. But we were so infatuated with one another that we didn't stop to think. As a matter of fact, we see now that we were drawn to one another because we suffer from identical psychiatric problems. We talked about these problems together and it seemed as though we were finding help for ourselves in a special and easy way. But it hasn't worked out. Our problems accentuated from the day of our marriage. We found that we were getting on each other's nerves. And now she can't take it any more."

I have of course known exceptions to the general rule. One of the happiest homes I know is where a young couple and their three children live. He loved her on first sight and told her the first time they met that he was going to marry her. Engagement? One month!

But this is the exception. This man of whom I write is a man of exceptionally quick judgment in everything he does. His marriage fell into the normal pattern of his life and everything has worked out beautifully. For most people, however, I think it's wise for them to know one another for at least a year and to be formally betrothed or engaged for at least six months. A six-month term allows the law of undulation to operate even within the magic and charmed circle of engagement. There is some wisdom in the old saying: "Marry in haste; repent at leisure."

Are there any special questions we should ask before engagement?

Yes! You should ask: "Am I really in love?" In true love there is a deep and unconditional yielding of devotion to another. Have

I this? Or am I only infatuated? Are my thoughts of the one to whom I am considering being engaged filled with respect and admiration? And is my friend interested in me and not in anything I possess or any gift I may have? Do we suit each other—temperamentally, emotionally, physically and socially? Is there likely to be any question in the future about religion? For any true Christian this should not be an issue, for naturally he will only marry within the circle of his fellow Christians. The commandment still stands: "Be ye not unequally yoked with unbelievers" (II Corinthians 6:14). Is there any physical ailment that would make marriage undesirable? And, of course, you will ask yourself: "Am I absolutely certain that God's blessing is on our intended union? Have we prayed together for guidance about His good and perfect will? Is it in His name that we are going to be joined as one?" If the answer to all these questions is "Yes," then go right ahead. There is every evidence that God is in it.

Is it wise to have holidays together while engaged?

Why not? Anything that affords you time to be in each other's company for longer periods is obviously useful. Avoid laziness, however. Avoid lounging around with no definite things to do. Make the most of your time together. Plan your days. See all there is to be seen in the countryside around. Visit friends together. Get them also accustomed to thinking of you as being meant for one another. Show them your Christian love for one another. Take time to pray with each other; this can be a very lovely and sacred bond between you. Anything on which you cannot ask God's blessing, avoid and put away. He will bless you for it.

What do you think about mixed marriages?

By mixed marriages, we usually mean "racially mixed" marriages. There are many different points of view on this issue.

For myself, I believe that race or color need not loom large as a problem in any Christian's mind. Some of the loveliest marriages I know are so-called "mixed marriages." When God gives some undeniable signs that your choice, though of another race or pigmentation of skin, is His choice, then don't hesitate.

It is well, however, for everyone in such a situation to ask some very basic questions. What you are about to do will affect not only you but your children after you. While it is impossible to state what are the problems that colored children from your marriage may face, it is very likely that they will be far greater than you personally ever faced. I do not know how this issue can be justly or accurately assessed. I come back to the need for a clear revelation of the will of God that this is what He has planned. When that is given, then there need be no further fear.

Love overleaps the barriers of race or caste. If God gives you this love, and if you can face all the questions of the last paragraph and find the answer to be affirmative, then hesitate no longer. You may have to face special problems with your parents and your family; but ultimately the decision is yours. Discuss everything freely and fully with some Christian couple whose judgment you have come to trust; or discuss it with the minister who is going to effect the union between you at the marriage service—that is, if you can trust him to be a truly spiritual guide and counsellor under God in such a matter: I have known ministers with whom I would not unbare my heart on a subject like this. Helpful discussion with a friend who will be truly Christian and absolutely objective should help resolve the doubts that may be lingering in your mind. If, on the other hand, you are very much in love, and yet feel that marriage is going to create very great problems, stop it before it is too late. Better to have a sore heart now than to bear a cross for the rest of life's way.

What reading should an engaged couple do together?

Well, this is hard to answer. Basically, what is being asked is, Can some book or books provide us with first-class advice on how to live a successful married life?

There are, of course, many books on this subject and I always have a supply of them on hand in our church library or near me when I am engaged in marriage counselling. I don't think there is any point in making a list of books for you to read, for in many ways it is best for you to make your own selection. Go down to your local library and ask the librarian to guide you on the books in stock on the shelves that deal with the nature of marriage and also with the "how-to" of all forms of married intimacy. You will be surprised at the wealth of material that is available to you in any of these local libraries. Unfortunately, some of the very best are out of print and this may require further search and some buying on your own. But believe me it will be well worth it.

The reason for advising such reading is the abysmal ignorance of so many adults about sex. In spite of the massed effect of millennia of study, education, culture and research, there is still a major vacuum in many minds on the nature of marriage, sex and all allied subjects. A research chemist may spend his day exploring the wonders of biological formations. At night he ponders his ignorance about homosexuality. We have seen man walk on the moon more than 230,000 miles away; but we know more of that than we do about our own genitalia. To be successful marriage must be based on knowledge. This is why engaged couples should set themselves to do some careful research into the challenging world they are soon to meet. A great number of first-class articles are published from time to time in good journals, and some libraries keep records on these. It may be very wise to ask your librarian friend if there is anything of that nature that he would recommend.

Anything else?

Yes! Read through every passage in the Bible together where there is reference to or where the subject of marriage is dealt with in depth.

It is amazing how much there is in the Bible about marriage. Some of the loveliest stories of courtship in any literature are found here too. God's laws on marriage should be marked very carefully. These should be among the first passages underlined in the family Bible. It would be good if the minister had time to go through such passages with those about to be wed. But generally speaking, there simply isn't time to do so; and it is sad that it should be so. Engaged couples should, however, set themselves to read the best they can find on the subject. Matthew Henry's commentaries on the great biblical passages are quite priceless. There is nothing dated or old-fashioned in what he has to say. It is germane and contemporary. Read the Bible; study the commentaries; and fill in the gaps with something just off the press. By the time this book reaches its readers many more books on this subject will have been written. Ask your librarian what's new in this field—especially what is written from a Christian standpoint. It will all help.

With this kind of knowledge and equipment you will come to your wedding day prepared as you really ought to be. The day of days will be all the more glorious if it finds you so informed and alerted. Knowledge is always power. Seek for wisdom; for wisdom is the principal thing. Then trust God for all the rest.

You will find He never fails.

3: The Wedding

How shall we choose the day?

At every point it is right that parents on both sides should be consulted. For them, it is a day of high hopes fulfilled; nothing should be done without seeking and finding their help.

This naturally applies to the choice of a wedding day. Business pressures can make it hard to fit the right day in—that is, what you may think is the right day. But there is nothing like an open conference attended by the parents to help in this. And please don't fix the day fully without ensuring that the minister is free to be with you. How often have I found a young couple come to tell me of their wedding plans, with everything arranged, reception suite and halls booked, and my datebook already filled to the breaking point on that very day! It is best to fix everything loosely with everybody before finalizing anything.

It is the normal practice in many parts of the world for the parents of the bride to be hosts on that day. Great consideration should be shown here. They may be in very modest circumstances and unable to supply the type of wedding banquet they would desire. This should be treated with tact and understanding, especially by the groom. Agreement should be reached in open conference as to the type of wedding being planned and the number of guests that may be invited. Otherwise, and this I have often seen, a man and his wife in their later years are plunged into debt in order to make a brave show to the world.

Nothing like this should be tolerated in a Christian wedding. Consideration for everyone should be the keynote of all the details. There may be some situations where it is impossible to have the kind of wedding you would wish because of some recent bereavement or because of some serious sickness of a beloved member of the family. Look the whole situation over completely and in the end, as you seek God's help, you will find all working for the best.

Who will form the wedding party?

This is a question that bride and groom alone can answer. It is usual to have a Maid or Matron of Honor in attendance on the bride and for other bridesmaids to be chosen as is deemed best. The groom will make his choice of Best Man and, in addition, ushers are normally chosen to share in the reception of the guests and to stand with the bridal party during the ceremony. It is the bride's prerogative to determine the size and composition of the party. Normally of course this is discussed together and certainly should be made a matter of prayer.

All of this is rooted far back in history. Psalm 45 is a lovely description of a wedding party, and it is as modern as anything in the twentieth century. For the bride, the wedding day is the day of all days—the day in which she is truly queen among her friends. Those chosen for the bridal party are usually taken from the inner circle of friends both of bride and groom and, if they really fulfill their office well, they can add much to the beauty and dignity of the occasion.

What about wedding vows? Should these be recited or said?

I much prefer to have the bride and groom make their vows to each other without the intervention of a minister. It is often customary for the minister to take the vows phrase by phrase and for the participants to repeat them. But this is really very childish. In discussions leading up to the wedding, time should be taken to consider the vows that will be exchanged with one another; and this should give ample time for the memorizing of them. In taking the vows, bride and groom should face one another, take each other by the right hand, and then quietly state in the hearing of all present the vows of holy wedlock. I have from time to time married couples who have developed, and that in a very lovely and solemn way, their own vows. Whatever is done, anything is preferable to repeating them by rote under prompting of the minister.

Sometimes this comes as an unexpected thought to bride and groom. They feel that in the excitement of the moment they may forget the lines they have to say, and they shrink back from what may be an added ordeal. But in general I have found that when they think the matter through, the couple agree that taking the vows in this way is far more mature and meaningful. I have always felt that the significance of the act of exchanging the wedding vows is greatly enhanced when this practice is followed. This applies to any statement that the bride and groom may make to one another during the ceremony—at the giving of the ring as well as at the giving of the marriage pledges.

I have been at weddings which seemed one great big show and I didn't like it. How can we make ours different?

How often has this question been asked of me! It certainly is true that in many cases a wedding is a time for levity, frivolity and triviality. This makes a mockery of any true marriage ceremony and should be ruthlessly avoided. Ultimately, everything depends on the attitude of the bride and groom. If you have made it your business to tell your friends that you are planning a really Christian wedding and that your one desire is that God will be honored at your wedding, then the battle is won before you start. As aids to worship, you should decide whether or no you wish to have congregational praise during the service; whether or no there will be a choir or soloist present—and if so be sure that what will be sung fits in with your ideal concept of your wedding day; and whether or no any other form of music should be performed. The bridal march itself can set the tone. You may decide to have something that is specifically Christian. When Queen Elizabeth II of England was married to Prince Philip she chose as the bridal music for her entry to the sanctuary "Praise My Soul the King of Heaven." Could any choice be more fitting?

Is it good to have photographs during the church service?

No! Nothing can be more distracting. My own principle has been to discuss this question with the bride and groom, agree with them that a sufficient number of pictures in the sanctuary should be taken either by the official photographer or attending friends, and then reach agreement with the photographer that from the commencement of the religious service his camera will be unused. Certainly most brides want a complete photographic record of their wedding day and it is natural that they should. But the clicking of cameras and the flashing of light bulbs, sometimes at the most solemn moments of the ceremony, are quite out of place. If the minister gives adequate time at the beginning for a full set of pictures to be taken of the party when fully grouped for the service; and if when the bridal party returns through the church to meet and greet their friends there is further opportunity to get full shots of the married couple, there should be no further need for the production of cameras. While the marriage license and other documents are being signed further shots can be taken and in this way a full coverage of everything essential is made. But by safeguarding the religious service from intrusion of any kind the sanctity of the occasion is undoubtedly heightened.

What documents are necessary for a wedding?

Every state or province has its own marriage license bureaus. It is necessary to obtain a marriage license, and frequently evidence of residence in the area needs to be supplied. Residential requirements vary from place to place. Be sure to check this out fully. A marriage license, however, is obligatory and this is only supplied after due notice has been given—again there are time variants from country to country. Some churches require that notice of banns should be given. Banns is an old word signifying notice of an intended marriage. It comes originally from the word "ban." By reading the "banns" on three successive Sundays opportunity is given for objections to and a possible "banning" of the proposed union. Some churches will only use a "banns" certificate as the marriage license, and this should be carefully looked into. Generally speaking, however, the Registrar of Marriages appointed by the City or State government will supply the document you need on payment of the prescribed fee.

In addition, most churches keep their own marriage register; this also should be signed after the marriage has been solemnized. All marriage documents should be witnessed by the signatures of two people—usually the Best Man and the Maid of Honor. A certificate of marriage is then given—a detachable section of the original marriage license; it goes without saying that this document, this certificate of marriage, becomes immediately one of your most valuable documents and should be safeguarded accordingly.

In what sense is marriage a mirror of Christ's union with His Church?

We get to the heart of the matter with this question. You will have studied the appropriate biblical passages with your fiancée before coming to your wedding day. Certainly this comparison is one of the most profound similes in all the Bible. St. Paul writes of this and uses the analogy with great force. Not once or twice but frequently. One of the greatest of his paragraphs on this subject is in Ephesians 5. He writes:

> Wives, be in subjection unto your own husbands, as unto the Lord. For the husband is the head of the wife, as Christ also is the head of the Church, being Himself the saviour of the body. But as the Church is subject unto Christ, so let the wives be to their own husbands in everything.
>
> Husbands, love your wives, even as Christ also loved the Church, and gave Himself up for it; that He might sanctify it, having cleansed it by the washing of water with the word, that He might present the Church to Himself a glorious Church, not having spot or wrinkle, or any such thing; that it should be holy and without blemish. Even so ought husbands to love their wives as their own bodies. He that loveth his wife loveth himself. For no man hateth his own flesh; but nourisheth and cherisheth it, even as the Lord also the Church. For this cause shall a man leave his father and mother, and shall cleave to his wife; and the two of them shall become one flesh.
>
> This mystery is great: but I speak in regard of Christ and His Church. Nevertheless, do ye also severally love each one his own wife even as himself; and the wife see to it that she fear her husband.

It is good to realize that even St. Paul recognized this as "a great mystery." For it is hard to believe that this marriage you are now planning is going to be, and that in a most fundamental way, an expression of the relationship Christ has to His Church. When this tremendous thought really grips you, there will be an added sense of wonder, a higher dimension of awe, in all your thoughts about your wedding. I have already said that some of Matthew Henry's commentaries on the great wedding passages have never been surpassed. Let me quote two sentences from him on this section from the Epistle to the Ephesians:

> As the Church's subjection to Christ is proposed as an exemplar to wives, so the love of Christ to His Church is proposed as an exemplar to husbands; and while such exemplars are offered to both, and so much is required of each, neither has reason to complain of the divine injunctions. The love which God requires from the husband in the behalf of the wife will make amends for the subjection which he demands from her to her husband; and the prescribed subjection of the wife will be an abundant return for that love of the husband which God has made her due.

You see from this how deep is the link between the bond of marriage which God ordained as one of creation's ordinances and the eternal purpose of God the Father for the union of Christ with His Church. You are indeed treading holy ground when you walk down the aisle towards your groom. To know that this is a partaking of the essential life of Christ in all its radiant fulness should add immeasurably to the joy of your wedding day.

Is there any other Bible passage we should specially remember on our wedding day?

There is one I like to stress and it is found in Hebrews 13:4. I like this translation of it the best of all. It reads: "Both honourable marriage and chastity should be respected by all of you. God Himself will judge those who traffic in the bodies of others or defile the relationship of marriage." From this it is clear that marriage should be an acknowledged norm among Christians. Anything of sexual intimacy that happens outside the marriage bond carries on it God's holy condemnation. "God Himself will judge those who . . . defile the relationship of marriage." In other words, sex outside of marriage is outlawed by God. If sexual relationships occur within the divinely ordered plan of creation, the only outflow is fulfillment and health. Sex, however, outside of marriage, practiced in isolation from the true union that God ordained for man and woman, and operating apart from the pattern so clearly outlined in the Bible, will bring with it sorrow, affliction and remorse.

Let me illustrate. Recently I was called on the telephone by a young man called Tom. He asked to see me and we met the same afternoon.

"I would like very much to get married to Mary," Tom said. "She is everything I could possibly desire. We have known each other now for about six months and there is no doubt in my mind that she is in love with me. Certainly I love her. But I've one tremendous hang up. Can I mention it?"

"Of course. Go on."

"Well, it's like this. I've been a Christian for a very short time—about nine months only. You know that, of course. But before that—and I've never mentioned this to you before—I really lived it up. I've slept with a lot of girls and have had every kind of sexual experience with lots of them. Looking back, I wish I could erase the whole thing; but I can't. And now that I've really found true love, true Christian love, and that with a girl I believe to be virgin pure, I feel so dirty and unclean that I can't see how I can ever ask Mary to be my wife. Can you give me any advice? Should I tell her all about this? Or should I let a blanket of silence fall across the past? I need your guidance. Can you help me?"

I thought for a while. Then I said, "It's inevitable that you should think as you do since you have given your life over to Jesus Christ. His ethic is now your ethic. It's natural too that you should hate yourself for the things you did in the past. But self-condemnation at this point is going to do no good. No! God has forgiven all your sin. That doesn't mean that you can forget about it—though God does forget. But it means that you can offer to Mary the possibility of marriage with one whom God hasn't cast out but has forgiven freely. There is no need for you to tell Mary your past history. Leave that with God. Offer your heart to her as you now are and pray that God will guide you into His perfect will."

There the conversation ended. In Christ's light he saw light. He was truly sorry for what had happened before. In the light of Christ he knew it was utterly wrong. Remorse and regret filled his mind. Yet God had received him and it was as a Christian, ransomed, healed, restored, forgiven that he at last was joined with Mary in the bonds of holy wedlock. And the word "holy" can't be overemphasized. It was indeed a sharing of the life of God; and that is a sharing of "His holiness."

Better by far if Tom had never lived as he did before. But I reminded him in our conversation that many of the New Testament Christians were just like himself, and Paul wrote to them, recalling without hesitation the kind of life they had previously lived—swindlers, impure, idolaters, perverts, thieves, foul-mouthed and rapacious—but he adds, with infinite tenderness and joy: "And such were some of you: but you are washed, you are sanctified, you are justified in the name of the Lord Jesus Christ, and in the Spirit of our God." This is the marvel of redeeming grace. It can cancel out the effects of sin and create newness of life in the image of the Son of God empowered by the Spirit of purity and love.

What about the reception?

If everything has gone according to plan, the place where the reception is being held should soon be reached. A good reception is determined by the amount of careful planning that is put into it.

The Best Man has major responsibility here of course. In conference with the ushers and others he should ensure that the guests are suitably welcomed on arrival, that the reception line at which most guests have their first opportunity for congratulating the married couple is carefully set up, and that there is no uncertainty anywhere as to where the guests should go after passing through the receiving line. Care should be taken to refuse the offices of official photographers at this point. I have seen a wedding reception held up for more than an hour while the photographer fussed around trying to get the ultimate in effect. With gentle tact, prepare all this beforehand and make certain that a minimum of time is wasted prior to the reception. After grace has been said, the meal is served; the bridal cake is cut at the appropriate time; and the time comes for some speech in honor of the bride. This can take the form of a toast, though that is not necessary. Usually, the person chosen to do this is someone who has known the bride for a long time and can speak factually and amusingly about her. Then comes the moment for the reply to this address. Here the groom for the first time has the chance to speak. If you are determined to make your wedding a truly Christian wedding, this occasion gives you a terrific opportunity to speak a good word for Jesus Christ. It can be made a real act of testimony. Some of the most exciting testimonies to the grace of God I have heard at wedding receptions. This may not be easy. But it is worth it ten thousand times over.

Ronnie was very hesitant about this. We had been going over all the plans of his wedding to Marilyn; and when I suggested that in response to the toast he should give a living testimony to Christ, he was visibly daunted. "My folks know that I don't dig the things they do. Most of my relatives will be there because they will be looking for lots of heavy drinking. I don't know just what the reaction will be if I introduce this kind of talk."

"Will you ever have a better opportunity to tell them about your new life in Christ?"

His brows puckered in thought. "No, I'm thinking that I might be taking an unfair advantage of them by speaking of Christ just then."

Marilyn broke in. "But Ronnie, some of them may never get another chance to learn what God can do. They knew you in the old days and they know there is a real difference now. Why not let them in on the secret? Why not tell them that it is our supreme hope to build a Christian home with God's help?"

There was another long and weighty silence. Then this!

"Okay, I will. You'll need to help me prepare what to say. But I'll do it."

And he did.

The memory of those tense moments when he braced himself after giving the normal thanks to all who should be thanked will never fade. In the simplest terms he spoke for God.

"You all know me and have known me for a long time. You have seen a different guy in the past year and I want to tell you what made the difference. Very simply I came face to face with Jesus Christ through the influence of a fellow student who came into our residence last Fall. He was from Germany. Almost as soon as he got into residence he began holding Bible study in his room, and one day he asked me along. Naturally I didn't go. You know that I wasn't interested in anything like that. But he kept asking till one day, for no reason that I can really give, I went along. That was the start for me of the most exciting trip I've ever taken. I went regularly to the little group, and one day I knew I must do something about Jesus Christ. I knew what I ought to do by then. And I did it. I took Christ and everything that He stands for—truth, purity, honesty, love and abundant life. And it's because of that I'm here today, for it was in that same study group I met Marilyn"

He spoke simply but with the eloquence of the heart. God helped him and that reception suddenly became like an ante-room of heaven.

This is the heart of a Christian wedding reception. If you really want to let everybody know what kind of life you propose to live together, then speak up and speak out for God on that day. You will never have cause to be sorry that you spoke the truth and bore your witness. There is always a special aura of golden light in any wedding reception that has this kind of witness to Christ at its heart.

Anything else?

There is really no end to what could be added to all that's gone before. But we have covered the basic things. You must make up your mind about serving champagne, wines or harder liquors. You must decide whether or no you wish to have liberty for smoking. Customs vary in many different parts of the world. But the decision of the bride and groom in this is absolute. Settle together what you are willing to tolerate. The rest you can safely leave in God's hands.

You can do that all the more readily if the first Guest invited to your wedding is the Lord Jesus Christ. It was at a wedding, you will recall, that He for the first time displayed His miraculous powers. And John says: "This beginning of miracles did Jesus in Cana of Galilee and manifested forth His glory, and His disciples believed on Him" (John 2:11). There is something very suggestive there. This "beginning" of miracles was only a "beginning." At a thousand thousand weddings since that time He has continued to show His miraculous powers. Where Jesus is, there is always joy. Where Jesus is, the best is always being made better. Where Jesus is, the best is ever kept to the last. If Jesus is not at the wedding, there is a blank bigger than the universe itself. Be sure to have Him with you at yours.

4: Christian Basics of Sex

Is there a real link between Christian theology and a Christian concept of sex?

Of course there is. It is one of the major misfortunes of the Church that, by and large, she has abdicated her position as God's teacher in this most vital of areas. When God made man He made them "male and female." He gave commandment to man to "be fruitful and multiply, and replenish the earth" (Genesis 1:28). Built into the very heart of the creation ordinances is sex. But I feel sure that at least 90 per cent of the married people in our churches today entered into marriage without having this clearly pointed out to them. God gave the gift of sex like a precious jewel to humanity—the crown of all His creation. "And God saw that it was good." This gleaming, pulsating, controlling and so satisfying a gift came from the One who only does wonderful things. As I have already said, the "imago Dei" in man is incomprehensible without giving the right place, and that means a very central place, to sex. Judaic and Christian teachings alike stress that "maleness" and "femaleness" together make "man"; and since sexual intercourse is at the very heart of the marriage bond, it is clearly by divine design that it is set at this most intimate of all relationships between "man" and "woman."

Our Lord stressed this when, in discussing divorce with the Pharisees, He went to the nerve center of the issue and said:

> Have you not read, that He which made them at the beginning made them male and female. And said, "For this cause shall a man leave his father and mother, and shall cleave unto his wife: and these two shall be one flesh?" Wherefore, they are no more two, but one flesh. What

therefore God hath joined together let not man put asunder.

Our Lord quotes here from the Genesis record. He openly states that this was "in the beginning." Sex therefore is the dream-child of God. The oneness of husband and wife is made complete when all other earthly associations are left behind and the "wife" cleaves to, holds fast to, is joined to, her "husband." Marriage is not consummated until sexual relationships have been established. And such relationships are holy, beautiful, pure and good.

Why has the Church kept silence on this?

I don't know. If every preacher were a true expository preacher, taking the Word of God systematically and ensuring that every great issue of life with which the Bible deals had similar coverage in his teaching ministry, this could not have happened.

The Bible is replete with references to sex and its place in the divine cosmos. Let me quote some of the great passages again—although I am not forgetting that you are supposed to have discovered all these for yourself and to have studied them. Look first at this unique passage from Proverbs 5:1-8, in which the strongest warnings are given about misuse of sex.

> My son, attend unto my wisdom, and bow thine ear to my understanding.
>
> That thou mayest regard discretion, and that thy lips may keep knowledge.
>
> For the lips of a strange woman drop as a honeycomb, and her mouth is smoother than oil;
>
> But her end is bitter as wormwood, sharp as the two-edged sword.
>
> Her feet go down to death; her steps take hold on hell.
>
> Lest thou shouldst ponder the path of life, her ways are moveable, that thou canst not know them.
>
> Hear me now therefore, O ye children, and depart not from the words of my mouth.
>
> Remove thy way far from her, and come not nigh the door of her house.

Read alongside of this the tremendous passage in Proverbs 7:1-27. Clear is the warning given. The house of the prostitute is the house of death.

> Let not thine heart decline to her ways, go not astray in her paths.
>
> For she hath cast down many wounded: yea, many strong men have been slain by her.
>
> Her house is the way to hell, going down to the chambers of death.

But Proverbs is not only negative: it has great positive advice to give. As for example in the following lines:

> Drink waters out of thine own cistern, and running waters out of thine own well.
>
> Let thy fountain be blessed: and rejoice with the wife of thy youth.
>
> Let her be as the loving hind and pleasant roe; let her breasts satisfy thee at all times; and be thou ravished always with her love (Proverbs 5:15, 18-19).

Nothing could be clearer than this. True sexual satisfaction is to be found by a young man with "the wife of his youth." As the desert traveller finds refreshment at the oasis where the well is deep and the water cool, so may man and wife be refreshed by one another. Sexual experiences are intended by God to this end—refreshment and joy. And God, says the writer of Proverbs, sees a husband and wife being thus helped and encouraged through their mutual intimacy and He is well pleased.

> The ways of man are before the Lord, and He pondereth all his goings (Proverbs 5:21).

Moving into the New Testament we find no change in the fundamental ideas. J. B. Phillips has a tremendous translation of St. Paul's counsel to the Church in Corinth. It is a passage that every Christian should know by heart. You find it in chapter 7 and from verse 2 onwards; here is part of it:

> It is a good principle for a man to have no physical contact with women. Nevertheless, because casual liaisons are so prevalent, let every man have his own wife and every woman her own husband. The husband should give his wife what is due to her as his wife and the wife should be as fair to her husband. The wife has no longer full rights over her own person but shares them with her husband. In the same way the husband shares his personal rights with his wife. Do not cheat each other of normal sexual intercourse, unless of course you both decide to abstain temporarily to make special opportunities for fasting and prayer. But afterwards you should resume relations as before, or you will expose yourself to the obvious temptation of the devil.

Paul here affirms and defends the mutual and equal sexual needs of both partners. It is gross folly to imagine that only the male has "rights" while the woman must remain passive and submissive. Recently a woman said to me: "Why does my husband love me only at night? During the day I long for some token of his love to me. But he never shows it. He needs a bed to show his love; and this somehow doesn't seem right." Of course this isn't right. And what Paul is stressing here is that in any true marriage, both husband and wife must consider one another to the fullest degree. It is only in such consideration that true joy will abound. Marriage is a great cooperative adventure, and nowhere more so than in the realm of sexual satisfaction. It is possible for either partner—though admittedly the male is the most frequent offender—to be utterly selfish in demand. This is not good. Indeed, it is expressly forbidden in the clear teaching of the apostle. And along with these lessons from this instruction given to the Corinthian Church this should be added. Spiritual growth and maturity are in no way impeded by normal sexual intimacy. Indeed, the latter can significantly aid the former. I have observed many frustrations among married couples through the dominance of one or other of the partners, a dominance that has expressed itself most vehemently in demand for sexual gratification. It is wrong for a husband to demand intimacy with his wife at a time when she is tired after a long day with the children; or when she is worried over some problem; or when she is feeling unwell. Yet I have known men who have beaten their wives during the evening and later demanded sexual intimacy. The beast in any of us is never far from the surface!

One more passage should be noted if we are to have a broad spectrum of biblical teaching on sex and marriage. Paul is writing to his beloved church in Thessalonica and he says (again I quote from Phillips):

> To sum up, brothers, we beg you and pray you by the Lord Jesus, that you continue to learn more and more of the life that pleases God, the sort of life we told you about before. You will remember the instructions we gave you in the name of the Lord Jesus. God's plan is to make you holy, and that entails first of all a clean cut with sexual immorality. Every one of you should learn to control his own body, keeping it pure and treating it with respect, and never regarding it as an instrument for self-gratification, as do pagans with no knowledge of God. You cannot break this rule without in some way cheating your fellow men. And you must remember that God will punish all who do offend in this matter, and we have warned you how we have seen this work out in our experience of life. The calling of God is not to impurity but to the most thorough purity, and anyone who makes light of the matter is not making light of a man's ruling but of God's command. It is not for nothing that the Spirit God gives us is called the *Holy* Spirit (I Thessalonians 4:1-8).

Purity is the goal of all true marriage. Sexual passion dare not determine the choice of a wife—that is what the pagans do and they have no true knowledge of God. Lust as such does not belong in the lexicon of any true Christian. No! God wills that through the intimate life of husband and wife we should grow in sanctification, we should become holy, we should become vessels fitted for His use. And in order to aid us in this great task God has given to us His *Holy* Spirit.

I have always thought that sex was "worldly," but what you are saying is the very opposite of this!

It certainly is. One of the reasons for this is that much of the knowledge you have gained about sex has come from rather questionable stories. You have been led to believe that much of it is really illicit and thereby prohibited to the Christian. Here again the Church stands condemned. We have not taught as we should have done. We have not allowed the brilliant beams of light that radiate from God's Word on this all-important subject to shine within our own minds. In all probability, we have not known that the Bible has so much to say on the matter.

Well, now is the time to get everything straightened out. You are launched on the most glorious and thrilling adventure of your life. God has blessed you as many others have not been blessed. See to it that you use His gifts to His glory, your own growth in grace, and the right teaching and helping of others.

It is very essential that the Christian basics of sex be understood by any young Christian couple entering marriage. You will never get a better textbook than the Bible on sex. All you need to know about gender and sexuality, about the true nature of the masculine and the feminine, about things erotic and things licentious, may be gathered by direct teaching from the Bible or by natural deduction from the principles it clearly outlines. There is no doubt that in many cases information about sex has been gathered from immodest and corrupt people. It is natural for the devil to corrupt the highest and he certainly has done that in the realm of sex. As a result, you may have heard plenty about free love, profligacy, prostitution, licentiousness, seduction, eroticism and fornication; and all you have heard may have left you with a perverted idea as to the real nature and glory of sex. You must be prepared to unlearn a great deal before you begin to know all that is worth knowing, and that means all that God has done in giving this most precious gift to man. And you must learn that it is "the pure in heart who see God" (Matthew 5:8). In God's book there is no alternative to purity, chasteness, virginity and virtue. It is to all such that His greatest blessings are given. Sex is supernatural in the truest sense of the term. It is God's own provision for man, for the perpetuation of the race, and for the mutual help and comfort that husband and wife may have for each other both in prosperity and adversity.

When you think again about sex, try to put away from you all thoughts of its being carnal and unspiritual, sordid and irreligious. There is in this gift of God to man the sharing of the divine nature in a very unique way. Marriage without sex is a tattered and empty thing. Where sex is given its true place in marriage, where husband and wife recognize that they belong to each other totally and that they should share all they have with each other totally, then a real beginning has been made towards a felicitous, joyous and successful union.

Why is it that sex has become in so many circles a dirty word?

Because of sin. There is no other reason. Sin defiles everything it touches. It taints everything it holds. This is what has happened in the case of sex.

The Bible is of course very explicit on this. The Bible traces everything back to God. This is its history of origins—God authors all! God is love and everything that flows from Him bears love's stamp upon it. All the attributes of God affirm His sovereignty and freedom, His omniscience, omnipotence and omnipresence. Everything has its beginning in Him. He made the sea and earth and sky. He made all kinds of living things in the sea, on the earth and for the air. "By faith we believe that the worlds were fashioned by the word of God so that our minds accept as fact that the whole scheme of time and space was created by God's commandment—that the world which we can see has come into being through principles which are invisible" (Hebrews 11:3, Phillips).

Now if this is so it follows that when He brought the physical and the human into existence, gave them the gifts of mind, memory and imagination, He gave them also this wonderful gem of sex. Marriage is by a similar divine ordination. In the first blush of creation's dawning, God "brought Eve to Adam" and "Adam knew his wife" (Genesis 4:1). The verb "know" as used here is a very tender yet comprehensive word to express the intimacy of the sexual relations they enjoyed. It is impossible to read the opening pages of the Bible, especially as they relate to the origin and creation of man, without noting that at the heart of everything marriage and sex are joined together. And God never intended it to be any other way. But when we reach the disastrous third chapter of Genesis and read the awesome story of

> man's first disobedience, and the fruit
> Of that forbidden tree whose mortal taste

> Brought death into the world, and all our woe,
> With loss of Eden

then the sin is seen that has corrupted everything since. You cannot really grasp the full significance of sin without noting the perversions that have encrusted themselves around this amazing blessing of sex. As I've said, sin tarnishes and blemishes, it corrupts and destroys all it lays its chilling fingers on. Hence the many perversions of the sex life in a society that still prefers its sin to obedience to God.

But one of the wonders of the new creation we find in Christ is that "all things become new." This is true of the full sex life of every believer in Christ. By His Holy Spirit He can instruct us how to use this gift to His glory; and, if we are willing to fulfill all His commandments, He will certainly make sex to become a wonderful agent of sanctification, cleansing and soul-unity in the home.

I have heard you say that marriage is the greatest bond of society. In what sense is this true?

Well, look at it this way. In Genesis 2:24, we read that "for this cause shall a man leave his father and mother and shall cleave to his wife; and they shall be one flesh." Here are a man and a woman about to be married. The Bible says that each of them will "leave father and mother." That is, they will separate from the home in which they have been reared, and establish their own home. In this way, a divinely created social unity—a new family—comes into being. In that new family, as children are born and reared, they will learn from parents who truly know God, the ways of God. The family thus becomes the basic unit of society —not the individual. And when you read on through the early records of God's dealings with a man like Abraham, you see very clearly that God thinks in family terms, not in individualistic terms. Before Isaac was born, God speaks to Abraham as though Isaac were already with him, and He shows the generations yet unborn that are to spring from him. When a nation ceases to recognize that the family unit is its greatest preserver, that households and not persons are its strongest bond, and that blood and kindred are the only true cradle for human personality, then that nation is facing great peril. The family is the foundation of human security, the true bastion of civilization, the social basis of the kingdom of God.

Should there be any exception to marriage being a permanent relationship?

Well, once again we must go to the Bible for our guidance. Our Lord said, "What therefore God has joined together, let not man put asunder" (Mark 10:9). This is a study that I'll want to take up again when we talk about divorce, but something should be said at this point when we are discussing the Christian basics of sex and marriage.

From the beginning of time, it is evident that monogamy was God's standard for man. Christian marriage requires a life-long association between one woman and one man. There is no other relationship that can adequately meet the complete needs of a family, besides the needs of the husband and wife.

If the relationship is not permanent, and children have been born, what a tragic world theirs immediately becomes. I often say that it is good for children to know their grandparents; for this gives them a deeper sense of rootage in the community, and with it comes a stronger sense of security, with the result that the child is all the better able to cope with the problems of life as he grows up to meet them. At the heart of much personal insecurity is the memory of an insecure home—a broken home. It is not right that children should grow into adolescence being pushed from one foster home to another. And yet how many such cases do we see every year! All people should know who their relatives are; and only fidelity in an abiding marriage relationship can make this possible. Every true marriage counsellor will therefore stress this soberly and with emphasis. For the sake of everyone concerned, a permanent one-flesh marriage bond is best. Nothing other than this can be regarded as being in the creative plan of God.

I suppose you mean that full personal realization is intended through marriage?

You couldn't have expressed it better. One of the great objectives of the Holy Spirit is that we should be "whole persons."

Many of us fail in this. We are all actors—good, bad or indifferent. But we do act parts and not least when it comes down to this all-important area of personal wholeness or fulfillment. The individual person is like a country over which we wander. Constantly we see new prospects before us. Continually we have the urge to attain to something higher than we have yet reached—but we generally refuse to be transparent. We want to seem what we are not. The result is that we become moulded into another character than we really want to be. At least so it seems to others—especially to our husbands or our wives, and sometimes most of all to our children.

One of our greatest needs is for utter honesty. This can come in a flash when we suddenly see the whole landscape of our lives. If this happens, the climate of our relationship with other people suddenly changes—and always for the better. Transparency of life and character is one of God's greatest gifts. And in marriage, we have the chance to approach to it very closely. This is one of our most privileged relationships.

How can this transparency be achieved in marriage?

Well, as I've said, the conditions could not possibly be better than in marriage. You are set apart to another and your life is knit in the closest bonds with another. You have therefore a prodigious capacity for developing the person and showing yourselves as you really are. You find an incomparable richness, a true and select dialogue in marriage, that is simply not possible in any other kind of relationship. There is of course a temptation constantly with us—namely, to act a part. Instead of following the course that will develop us as "persons" we camouflage our true selves and emerge as "personages." In the early days of courtship, engagement or marriage, it may seem best to tell your fiancee everything. But changes come. True dialogue has not really begun. And when it does, things can be very different for two persons who face one another then and bring everything in the past—upbringing, view of life, failings, customs and habits, idiosyncrasies and peculiarities—out into the open. Very soon you find that you are less alike than you thought. This is one of the most critical moments in any marriage. Be warned. Be prepared.

Of course, as I said when we were talking about the engagement period, you will have had opportunities already to see through to the essential "you" in either case. But real confrontation normally awaits the state of marriage. It is then that the two utterly different psychologies—the man's and the woman's—face one another and something has to be done about it.

Well, what is best? What will promote the greatest unity?

Utter transparency of character. No acting. No camouflage. But this is seldom found. If the right kind of sex-relationship is developing, if both husband and wife are finding true fulfillment in sexual relationships, the situation is a thousand times more hopeful. But let there be just one little quirk in that department and personality clashes are frequent. What happens is that either one will dominate the other, and this means that true dialogue is aborted and self-determination is paralyzed, or else one of the partners says to the other: "This is conduct which I find very difficult to understand." The result of this is that true dialogue is again broken and a flight from reality has begun in earnest. Much of this is of course done without any thinking through of the consequences. But the result is equally disastrous. The holding back of confidences becomes normal. Bit by bit each partner to the wedding becomes an island. Ultimately, communication can cease completely. Talk about separation and divorce begins to enter conversation.

Now all this is very sad. In some homes you find that transparency in walk and conversation before and with one another can be blocked out through the very noble desire to safeguard affection. The wife may say to herself: "I don't dare talk about that subject with my husband. It irritates him. If I raise it, we will certainly be quarrelling before night fall. Both of us will say things that we don't really mean or intend." But the end result will be further estrangement. How often have I seen this! It is happening in every part of your city. You may be sure that there are homes in your church in which this is quite a commonplace thing. Too bad!

The answer of course is to determine never to allow pretense or acting a part to enter your marriage relationship. That is easier said than done. It is so true that all the world's a stage and all the men and women merely players. The world is one big theater.

And in the circumscribed circle of the home, wife and husband can live a life of pretense with one another. Some succeed in carrying this through to the end. But the result is that there is no real dialogue, no true conversation of heart with heart, no intimate binding into one to the point where instinctively you know and agree with what your life-partner is thinking and planning.

Paul Tournier is most helpful in discussing this. In *The Meaning of Persons* he says:

> Even in the happiest marriage personal contacts cannot be a permanent state, acquired once and for all. The windows of the house have to be cleaned from time to time if the light is to penetrate. They get dirty more quickly in town, but there is no countryside so remote or so clean that they do not gradually lose their transparency. Between man and wife, too, the true dialogue has periodically to be re-established by the true confession of some secret; and the higher and more sincere our ideal of marriage, the more irksome it is to admit that we have hidden something.
>
> What we said about secrets is true in the domain of sex: there is a double movement, first of retreat and then of self-abandonment. The true meaning of modesty is to be found in this retention of a secret which will one day be handed over to the person of our choice, with whom it will thereafter constitute an unbreakable bond, a commitment. Without perhaps knowing anything yet of the distant goal of her instinct, a young girl begins to feel reluctant to undress in front of her parents. The latter sometimes think that this modesty in regard to them is silly. They are making the same mistake, and doing the same damage to their daughter, as in violating a secret.
>
> The appearance of this sense of shame is, in fact, the birth of a new person. And later the great engagement of life, self-determination, will be marked by the handing over of the secret, the gift of the self, the disappearance of shame.

In marriage, the moral dialogue must never be given up in place of the mere feeling of unity which the sexual bond gives. The reverse is the case. Christian basics of sex demand the full encounter of personalities. They must never be made an excuse for the easy road of physical love and nothing more. Out of true transparency in sexual intimacy a true person should grow.

Do you think this to be one of the real purposes of sexual pleasure?

Of course I do. This is one of God's supreme ways of binding husband and wife together—and that in a total oneness. Marriage is a great school of the person. It entails a high level of personal commitment. It entails also an exacting quality of intimate dialogue. This is one reason why sexual intercourse outside of marriage is an abdication of the person, for it takes place without any real constraint of personality. By marriage, God links man and woman in one. He makes them in this way into an effective team for His service. Life-long and permanent relationships are established on the firmest of foundations when husband and wife find together true fulfillment in sexual intercourse. Sexuality, in other words, is never an end in itself. It is intended to bind two lives together in such closeness and fusion that they will act out what they really are—that is, "one." If you look at this from another point of view, you can't help seeing that extra-marital sex is an utter violation of God's intent. It is a breach of a basic law of life. What is given in order to merge and amalgamate two persons in an indissoluble bond is being abused for ignoble and purely selfish ends.

To this we should add another element in true sexual intimacy. It is this. Both man and woman are equally motivated mentally and emotionally towards sexual cohabitation. It is simply not true that the man is more ardent than the woman, that women are colder than men. True sex is unitive. Marriage and sex are therefore joined together in the most absolute way. The continuing practice of sexual relationships between husband and wife tends therefore to unite at ever deeper levels those whom God has joined in one. Fulfillment for each should be sought by each. It is not right for a husband to use his wife as a means of sexual release. If there is true union, the husband will consider his wife. This will involve setting her interests before his own. By every means in his power he will see to it that he does not ask from her what she cannot give at a given time or hour. At no point more than in the moment of sexual relationship should these words apply:

> Put on therefore as the elect of God, holy and beloved, patience and tolerance, kindness, humility of mind, acceptance of one another and self-control. Forbearing one another, and forgiving one another . . . (Colossians 3:12,13).

If this is the attitude of mind that each brings to this exalted moment, then there is going to be a greater unity, which will show itself in love and consideration for each other. The wife will feel she is needed and that her husband cares for her. The husband will know himself loved and served with a devotion he never expected. And from all this God will be glorified. Nothing less than this should be expected from sex in the bonds of marriage.

I suppose the home also will show this unity?

Your supposition is correct. I recall two sitting before me in my office. Seven years had passed since I had married them. They had asked for the interview, and I sensed that things were going wrong. "It's like this," Joan said. "We have four children. You know them all and they know you well. Your name is a household word with us. But lately—oh, perhaps for the past nine months or so—Bert and I seem to be drifting apart from one another. I know I'm tired. I get annoyed with the children and find myself scolding them for the least thing. Supper is always a scramble—making the little one take her food, keeping the others from running all over the place, and watching the weather signals on Bert's face as to whether the day has been all right with him or no. During the day I find myself envious of Bert. He's away downtown, meeting all sorts of people, and I'm stuck here with the children. And by the time Bert does get home I'm ready to walk out. I know our home shouldn't be like this, but that's the situation today. And we can't go on."

I looked at Bert.

"I don't know what to say," he responded. "We've tried to keep everything right about Bible reading and evening prayer and things like that. But, of late, we sure seem to be drifting apart."

I hesitated to say anything; but eventually I said: "Let's put spiritual considerations aside for a moment and let me ask you how you are faring in your sex relationships with each other."

Quite unknown to me I had put my finger on the real issue. Joan was tired, no doubt about it. Because of this, when Bert and she reached bed she could give him none of herself, nor did she want what he had to give. I suggested taking a vacation, lazing in the sun with the children, discovering one another anew. Thank God, it worked. The tension-filled home changed back again to a place where love reigned. Ease, rest, fulfillment came. For God showed them again the wonder of their essential oneness. He showed them again their unity with Himself. And He took them again into love's high places and they brought back love with them, which spilled over in the home as they worked and laughed and slept.

The life of a child is bent by the quality of his parents' life and love. Families are blessed in ways they cannot understand when their father and mother "know each other" in the bonds of love's highest and holiest intimacy.

Do you believe it is possible for us in our twentieth-century Western civilization to maintain virginity until marriage?

I do. There are of course temptations on every side. The modern theater and our current movie productions are regularly exalting free love and sexual promiscuity. The great landmarks of morality which for generations guided people in our Western culture are largely ignored today. The result is that many find themselves faced with decoys and seductions which prove well-nigh irresistible. Siren songs of enticement can be heard with recurrent frequency. The "Playboy" philosophy of Hugh Hefner is a multi-million-dollar business; and there are ministers of the gospel who frequently write for its pages. The simple fact is that the tide is running swiftly against any fellow who is determined to maintain virginity until he can offer an unbroken chastity to his bride in marriage.

But it can be done. This is the wonder of the strength of God. Grace reigns. "Where sin abounded, grace did much more abound" (Romans 5:20). The promise of God is very definite: "Sin shall not have dominion over you" (Romans 6:14). There are many—far more than you and I probably realize—who are determined to keep themselves pure. Thank God for this! "He is able to succour them that are tempted" (Hebrews 2:8); and "He is able to keep you from falling" (Jude 24). Yes, you can win through—with God's help. Try it and see.

5: Sexual Adaptation

Can you give advice on how we can best become sexually adjusted to one another?

Surely! You must talk about sexual matters before marriage. One of you should open the discussion, whichever of you is most eager to have the situation talked over fully. What is vital is that a couple intending marriage should discuss with each other what they hope through their union to obtain and to give in the realm of sex. During your engagement, you will naturally discuss a thousand things. Don't leave this question unasked or undiscussed.

It is possible of course that in many cases there may be a very definite reluctance to raise this question of sexual relationships. But if you have followed us this far in our question and answer text, you should realize that sex is in the sight of God a very beautiful and sacred thing. Sex only becomes wrong when it is abused or misused. It certainly cannot be overemphasized that right and true knowledge of everything that deals with sex should be acquired by an engaged couple. Only so will they obtain the necessary factual information that will lead to the best kind of sexual adaptation in marriage.

The ignorance on this whole field of life is staggering. One can scarcely believe how closed the book of sex is to many. It is a *terra incognita,* an unexplored continent, an unknown discipline. All the more reason that in your case, since you are frankly discussing the whole matter with me, you should not shrink from asking anything that you think is relevant. You may have heard all kinds of tales at times about various types of perversion in sex. Items in the press may have made you wonder about all that is involved in the union of two lives and two bodies and their consequent fusion into one. It is good, I think, for married people to know not only what is right and good in sex, but also to know the deviations, the debasement and the misuses of sex. We may have time and space to elaborate on these later. Meantime, whatever else you do, get the facts and agree with one another what you are looking for in this area of life when you are married.

Is this kind of discussion often carried through by engaged couples?

Unfortunately, no! As a matter of fact, I have met with repeated cases of married couples who have never discussed the question together.

Some time ago in the office of a psychiatrist I encountered a couple who had never had sexual relations after thirteen years of marriage. This may sound absolutely incredible, but there are far more than you realize who are totally ignorant not only of the facts of life, but of what each can give the other through this means.

Selfishness can hold a man back from opening up the subject. Fear can keep a girl from frankly sharing her hopes and dreams with her husband-to-be. The reasons given are multiple. But the result is always tragic. Indeed, I can think of a number of homes where there has been total nervous breakdown both with husbands and with wives; and I am certain that the basic reason why they came to that state was their failure to open up the whole area of their sexual needs to one another and a consequent failure to get the necessary help before it was too late. The most important fact is that husband and wife are accountable to one another for meeting each other's needs. A husband should know how to arouse his wife tenderly and with great love to the point where she has a full sexual experience in the climax known as orgasm. Similarly the wife should help her husband and induce for him the same type of climax. The husband must give all conjugal rights to his wife, and so should the wife to her husband. When love is motivating all, this is a most natural and healthy procedure. When love is drawing the one nearer to the other, it will be love that will effect the desired objective. But, I repeat, this should be fully discussed with one another before you reach your wedding day. You must become knowledgeable in this entire area. It will repay you a thousand times over to do so.

What are the most essential facts that we should know?

First of all, you should realize that sexual relationships between husband and wife are like a duet played with two totally diverse instruments. Synchronization, harmony, tempo, rhythm, concord, attunement and musical score must all be perfectly matched in each instrument with the other. So it is in the case of the true fulfillment of union between wife and husband. Take the question of "tempo." Possibly this is one of the most important points to note. Let me try to make myself clear.

A man is normally aroused faster sexually than a woman. He can reach orgasm in a matter of minutes—sometimes even less than a minute. In course of time, he can become adept at controlling himself and withholding climax. Some wives think this facility on the part of a husband is very selfish, but it is simply the nature of a man to be so. And every wife should know it. On the other hand, a woman reaches orgasm much more slowly than a man. It is simple fact that it can take a woman from ten to fifteen times longer than a man to attain to orgastic fulfillment. Here therefore is a clear dilemma for both partners. There are many variables in this whole area of timing or tempo and it becomes incumbent on each one involved to consider the other and ensure, if possible, that complete fulfillment be attained in the sex act.

It would be very easy for either one to become annoyed with the other. And such annoyance is at the heart of a great deal of dissatisfaction within marriage. But when a couple understand this difference in tempo, and when they set themselves to prepare in such a way that the difference is allowed for and full consideration given to it, then it is very possible for husband and wife to reach orgasm simultaneously. What I am simply saying is that each partner must know the other in this most intimate sense, must accept it, go along with it, must become co-efficient if this intimacy is to be the blessing God means it to be. It may require great restraint on the part of the husband. It may necessitate a very definite fixation of purpose in the mind of the wife for a considerable period of time. But, at all costs, the variables of tempo should be known, observed and obeyed.

Now, what next?

I called the first great problem one of tempo. I call the second great factor one of design. To understand, you must let me refer to the nature of the body that God has given us, this body "so fearfully and wondrously made." At the upper meeting point of the inner lips which cover the female vagina is the clitoris. This is the center of all sexual sensation in women. It is a labyrinth of nerve cells and fibers all mingled and crowded together into very miniature proportions. There is a covering or prepuce over the clitoris, and if the covering of the clitoris is gently massaged or stroked back and forth over the clitoris, sexual desire is gradually stimulated. No woman will ever attain sexual orgasm without stimulation created by direct physical contact.

Now note carefully the following detail. When the male penis enters the vagina from a man-above position, the angle of penis to vagina is slightly from a lower to a higher point. The penis in this way will not naturally touch the clitoris; and this is of crucial consequence. In order to ensure sexual arousal and fulfillment, those nerve endings in the clitoris must be stimulated by the penis moving back and forth within the vagina. If there have been careful and endearing preparations towards this point, and if the penis enters the vagina at the time point when the woman has been sufficiently stimulated, there should be no difficulty in ensuring complete fulfillment for the wife—and for the husband too. The clitoris in a normal woman is about 1¼ inches from the entrance to the vaginal passage. If this is visualized clearly, then the process of final stimulation by the moving or rubbing of the penis over the clitoris becomes easy and facile.

In preparation for copulation, and in order to ensure that the wife is being helped in every way by her husband, it is a common recommendation that the husband adopt straightforward stimulation of the clitoris by a gentle holding of the clitoris in and through his fingers for whatever time is necessary to bring the wife to the point where she is ready for full intercourse. There is nothing unnatural about this. It is one of the tender duties that true love can provide. It is the way God has made us and whatever He has ordained must be good. The importance of carefully following through these primal details in the total act of sexual intercourse cannot be overestimated. The full orchestration in total symphony of body joined to body is known only where and when these details are watched and fulfilled. As one very wise man has put it: "Marriage is that relation between man and woman in which the independence is equal, the dependence mutual, and the obligation reciprocal."

Where is the biblical warrant for what you have just said?

At a host of places. But I always turn especially to the third chapter of Peter's first letter. There he gives a word to married Christians which is most relevant. Let me quote it fully from the Phillips version; it goes from verse 1 to verse 7.

> In the same spirit you married women should adapt yourselves to your husbands, so that even if they do not obey the Word of God they may be won to God without a word being spoken, simply by seeing the pure and reverent behavior of you, their wives. Your beauty should not be dependent on an elaborate coiffure, or on the wearing of jewelry or fine clothes, but on the inner personality—the unfading loveliness of a calm and gentle spirit, a thing very precious in the eyes of God. This was the secret of the beauty of the holy women of ancient times who trusted in God and were submissive to their husbands. Sarah, you will remember, obeyed Abraham and called him her Lord. And you have become, as it were, her true descendant today as long as you too live good lives and do not give way to hysterical fears.
>
> Similarly, you husbands should try to understand the wives you live with, honoring them as physically weaker yet equally heirs with you of the grace of life. If you don't do this, you will find it impossible to pray properly.

This is a very significant passage. It gathers up everything that we have emphasized in this whole area of becoming adjusted sexually to one another—and you will note that Peter stresses that the only true kind of adjustment is that in which the husband "honors his wife." I have always felt it most meaningful that at the end of this section he states that prayer can be hindered if there isn't this right relationship between husband and wife. That is a very solemnizing thought. Prayer has many facets and most of these facets have been caught by the great hymnwriters, but this particular point is one that is often missed. Given a wrong relationship at home, given a tension-filled house without anything of the true love of Christ shed abroad inside it, you can be sure that prayer offered there is not going to be heard. The reason is that the wrong conditions obtain. Prayer is answered when it is offered in the Name of Christ. But you cannot rightly offer prayer in that Name if you are openly denying the Name by dishonoring the wife to whom you are bound. And this should never be forgotten by parents who have the care of children. Prayer on behalf of our children is nullified, negated, aborted, if we are not living in the right sexual relationship with wife or husband. Whatever else may be stated about the value of maintaining right relationships with your life partner, never forget this one point that God by the Holy Spirit stresses so emphatically here: "Your prayers may be hindered."

I liked that phrase "Heirs with you of the grace of life." Can you say something more about it?

I'll be delighted to do so. I think you know that my custom is to give a verse from Scripture to every married couple on the day of their wedding and to expound it for two or three minutes during the wedding service. I always make a practice also of writing it into the marriage booklet from which we take the customary vows; this ensures that in days to come when they look back on their wedding day—and who doesn't frequently?—they don't have the chance to forget the message that was given them then.

Well, I think it would be true to say that I've used this verse more frequently than any other. It is one of the loveliest thoughts about marriage that can be found anywhere in the Bible. When two Christians are bound in holy matrimony, they become "heirs together of the grace of life." Grace is the only foundation on which we know life eternal, for "by grace you are saved." And the two who are made one—how strange God's arithmetic is: one plus one makes one—become heirs together of all God's wonderful fulness.

This word "together" is one to be stressed. We will talk more about it later. But it should be noted at this point. Togetherness is an absolute thing in all true marriages. The believers of the New Testament are always seen "together"—they assemble together, pray together, sing together, are comforted together, grow together, are knit together, reason together, sow together, reap together, travail in pain together, labor together, go together into the house of prayer, are gathered together. And what is true of the Church in general should be true of the Church in the home where wife and husband are one with each other, are "heirs together of the grace of life."

There are times when sexual intimacy is impossible. What advice do you give?

There is a normal monthly period when a woman because of menstrual flow cannot countenance sexual relations. There is a period before the birth of a child when it is obviously unwise to continue such relations—let the doctor advise you on this. A good doctor will always be able to help you in a host of situations. Get one whom you can trust. Unfortunately, on the North American Continent at least, the old custom of having a family doctor is rapidly vanishing. You now go to a clinic where there is one specialist in heart, another on blood, a third on surgical procedures, yet another will deal with gynecological problems, and so on. The old custom was excellent. You knew the doctor and he knew you. But if you can find a doctor to whom you can readily go, don't hesitate to ask the kind of question indicated above. There are, in fact, plenty of occasions when sexual relations are just not possible. What do you do?

If God is consulted, and I assume you will have done this, it may well be that this cessation from such relations will have nothing but a beneficial effect. There is no reason in the world why each party to a marriage should not practice continence when required. During periods of war, men are rudely separated from their wives for long periods of time. What should they do? Avail themselves of help from others? Never! The wedding promise that you "will faithfully keep yourself for him/her alone" is an unbreakable promise. God will guide you wisely. Commit the problem to Him.

Yet I have known men who have forced themselves on wives who were seriously ill. One can have only contempt for such behavior. I believe that whatever our God ordains is right. He will show you the right way. Abstinence from anything for a time is always a test of moral character. Let it be so here. And meantime remember with joy those times you have been together. All that is surely theme for great and joyful praise.

Praise for the joy of loving,
All other joys above;
Praise for the priceless blessing
Of love's response to love;

Prayer that the full surrender
Of self may perfect be,
That each be one with other,
And both be one in Thee.

Grateful memory will solace many an inevitable period of abstinence.

Can you give us any idea of how frequently intercourse is had by married people?

There have been many studies of this. I have made my own, and on general lines it agrees with the researches of others. Here, then, are some general observations.

Naturally, intercourse is more frequent in the first years of marriage. This generally settles down to about twice a week, or even less. Some couples have relations daily; but this is uncommon. After any period of separation from one another, there is usually an urge for more frequent intercourse—daily and possibly even twice a day.

My own poll taken some time ago showed the following record. Out of a total of ninety-nine couples polled, a very small number (about 2 per cent) had a sexual experience daily. About a third went for intercourse every two days and a little more than a third every three days. Of the remainder, 18 per cent averaged once every four days, and 12 per cent every five days or longer.

In general the husband seeks intercourse slightly more frequently than the wife; although, interestingly enough, if sexual relationships are carried on into later years in marriage—and there is of course no reason whatsoever why they should not be—the wife may well become more demanding than the husband.

What is all-important is that love should determine every decision. At no point should sexual relations ever be indulged in unless there is the fullest concurrence of both parties. Otherwise, look out for disaster. There is no sadder part in marriage counselling than endeavoring to placate a wife who has, as she might put it, "had enough." Vividly I recall Adrienne sitting before me and talking haltingly about her love life—or lack of it—with Harold. "He never considers me at any time. I must be ready to do his bidding at any hour of the day or night. I've known him to rouse me out of sleep—a drugged sleep at that, for the doctor had given me librium for sedation—and force me to let him use my body as he needed it. Is this what marriage is all about? Shouldn't there be some mutuality about this? I've got sex drives just as much as he has; but there's a time and place for everything and often I'm just not in the mood. He seems to be in the mood for it all the time."

I told her a lot of the things that I've been telling you, and she said she would discuss the problem with Harold at the first opportunity. She did. She did it quietly and after prayer. She suggested that they both see me and talk the whole thing through, and they did. I repeated much of what I had already said to Adrienne, and they left with a better understanding of how gloriously satisfying sexual relationships could be when entered into with mutual consent and joy. It has been good to watch this couple mature in every way and to see their home become a place where love is found. Harold's real problem was ignorance. No one had ever discussed with him the real nature of married relationships. He understands now. Every one of his friends has seen a marked change. But nobody knows where and how the victory was won.

What is meant in the Bible by the word "helpmeet"?

This word occurs in the second chapter of Genesis. God uses it. "It is not good for man to be alone; I will make an helpmeet for him." The Hebrew phrase means "a helper who is perfectly suited for him." Even more literally it could be translated "a helper as his counterpart." Whatever kind of translation you take, the meaning is simple and yet profound. The true idea of a woman's relationship to her husband is shown here. She is his counterpart, his complement, his mate. Only when this is realized in marriage is God's sovereign purpose being fulfilled.

> For woman is not undeveloped man
> But diverse:
>
> Not like to like, but like in difference.
> Yet in the long years liker must they grow.
>
> Till at the last she set herself to man,
> Like perfect music unto noble words;
>
> Distinct in individualities,
> But like each other ev'n as those who love.

The Genesis narrative is pictorial and highly picturesque. But it is in no way allegorical. The various pictures that are shown are expressive of actual facts. And when the biblical record says "she shall be called woman because she was taken out of man," it is portraying the foundation of an intercourse that was pure and blessed, without sin and without shame, so that the two, blameless and fearless, walked together in the sight of Him who made them for one another, and made both of them for Himself. I never read this Genesis narrative without being reminded of a comment by Matthew Henry. "Woman was taken out of man's side," he writes, "to suggest her equality with him; not out of his feet to imply inferiority, or out of his head to suggest superiority, but out of his side, implying companionship and equality." All this is involved in the word "helpmeet." And happy is the woman who understands what a place of glory this is.

Would you call marriage one of God's masterpieces of creation?

I don't see how you could do better. The question of sex is one of the problems as yet unsolved (and in all probability unsolvable) by the science of our times; and one might well ask if science itself could have given a more religiously fitting account of the physiological and biological facts as they are known to us. Sex is an absolute mystery. And marriage is like a watchman or sentinel over the sacredness of sex. Certainly, when the Bible stresses the interdependence that is at the heart of both sex and marriage, it is affirming one of the greatest truths affecting our lives. We cannot do without one another. We were never meant to live in isolation. This is what God stresses here. Fulfillment of life is found in self-giving; and no clearer symbol of this is obtainable than the holy institution of marriage. In marriage we learn that husband and wife need one another. The duties of family life demonstrate that we are bound together in the bundle of life in such a way that we cannot be segregated from one another. Seclusion of that type would destroy the race. Withdrawal, aloofness, separation and isolation have no part in God's plan for the human race. Indeed, it would not be stressing things at all if we were to affirm that the quality of interdependence that is at the heart of marriage is intended to be spread to other fields of human association. In this sense, marriage becomes a standard or an ideal for all mankind. God created them "male and female," and in doing so He showed the very basics of life to be love, self-sacrifice, givingness and generosity. This is one of the great lessons man needs to learn. Without it, we continue to pursue ends that are selfish, mercenary, worldly-wise and egotistic. The basic rules for sexual adaptation of man and woman and woman and man are equally basic for the tribes and nations of the earth. Where love is, selfishness dies. Can you imagine what the world would be like if those qualities that we have been speaking about were found in the parliaments of the world?

6: The Anatomy and Physiology of Sex

I think the time has come for you to tell us about the physical differences between man and woman. Will you?

Yes, the time has come. I certainly don't intend to make this an exhaustive treatise on the human body. What I would like to do is give the elementary and basic facts; but I want to do so quite candidly and thoroughly, for "a little learning is a dangerous thing." Where would you like me to begin?

Why not carry on from the points you mentioned when we were discussing "tempo" and "design"?

All right. When we talked about the difference in design between man and woman I spoke about the male penis and the female clitoris. Let's go back to that point.

The penis is set outside a man's body where the thighs are joined to the trunk. Through it runs a canal called the urethra, along which passes urine from the bladder and, at the appropriate time, seminal fluid. It is impossible for semen and urine to pass at the same time. When seminal fluid is passing, the body with marvellous efficiency closes all exit from the bladder.

Behind the penis is the scrotum, a loose pouch of skin containing the testicles, the two egg-shaped bodies which produce spermatozoa, the male reproductive gametes. Before birth, the testicles lie within the abdominal cavity; but shortly before birth they descend into the scrotum, and in all normal men remain there.

The testicles, those most unusual glands that secrete spermatozoa in the male body, also produce a hormone which is constantly absorbed into the body. The effect of this hormone becomes apparent at the time of puberty, when a boy begins to change into an adult. Hair grows on his face and body, and his voice breaks. The spermatozoa or sperm (the word "spermatozoa" is derived from two Greek words–*sperma*, meaning seed, and *zoe*, meaning life) are part of a fluid called semen, resembling for all the world the white of an egg. In a normal ejaculation, there are about 4,000,000,000 sperm. Such is the incredible marvel of life-giving potentiality stored within a man's body.

It is possible for the channels that hold and carry the sperm to become overloaded and frequently, especially during youth, the body may discharge the overflow. This usually happens at night in what are known as nocturnal emissions. These are often accompanied by dreams of a sexual nature together with a swelling of the penis, or erection, as it is more commonly known.

Erection of the penis is essential for sexual relationships between man and woman. What happens is this. As sexual arousal takes place, nervous signals cause the filling valves of each penile reservoir to open and blood pours into these chambers. Now, since these chambers are held in place by connective tissue, as they distend the penis becomes stiff and raises itself. A very delicate system of pressure detectors keeps the pressure at the right balance at all times, thereby ensuring that the erection is neither too much nor too little. All this is possible because of the presence of the series of small reservoirs that lie just under the skin of the penis and resemble rubber balloons. The operation of filling these blood vessels and valves is controlled by a network of nerves which would be the envy of any road engineer cutting a highway through a densely populated district. The nerves run directly to the spinal cord and to the brain. This control center monitors all impulses in each direction, from penis to brain and spinal cord and from the central nervous system to the penis.

This happens in every case?

It does. Penile erection is one of the extraordinary miracles of the human body. But I must invite you to pay the closest attention to what now follows. In the moment of sexual intimacy, the penile erection has taken place and it is always at the right angle for entry to the female vagina–another miracle. We certainly are, as I've said already, "fearfully and wonderfully made." As the penis enters the vagina and as intercourse progresses, a constant flow of nerve impulses speeds between the sexual organs and the body's central nervous system. Every other stimulus is made a part of the system. Proximity to one's partner, touching and fondling her, promotes a still more rapid buildup. The pressure mounts higher and higher until there is, in effect, an actual explosion.

This is the critical point in sexual intercourse for the male. At this point which I have called explosion, ejaculation takes place. As already noted, the urethra is immediately and automatically sealed off so that no urine may pass accidentally. In this moment of crisis and sublimation, the body throws a powerful pump into operation which pours forth about a quarter of an ounce of seminal fluid. As soon as this emission has occurred the climax is over and usually the penile erection ceases. This whole process for the man is called an orgasm.

Meantime, what about the woman?

If the arousal of which we spoke earlier has taken place, the entrance of the penis should result in the vagina's being ready to receive the penis. There is no need for any special preparations to aid entrance. The female body itself secretes adequate lubricants. And as the penis massages the labia, the vagina and the other related organs, the result should be true orgasm.

During orgasm, every segment of the woman's body quickens. Heart rate can reach 160 to the minute. Blood pressure can double. All the sensory nerves of the pelvic area move at breakneck speed. Sensations of all kinds, infinitely pleasurable, reach from the vulva, the vagina and clitoris through the entire nervous system. Waves of feeling cascade through the entire body. Then, as the orgasm recedes, a great sense of relaxation courses through the whole body.

Are orgasms repeatable? Or is one only to be expected?

When a man has one orgasm, he cannot have another until some time has elapsed. This is common to all men. It is different with women. Generally speaking, one orgasm may be satisfying enough; but there are many women who need and seek more than one at one time. Fortunately, for women this is possible. Indeed, given time and total relaxation, there is scarcely a limit to the number a woman may have.

This is a factor which husband and wife should establish. It won't take much clinical research to learn how many orgasms any wife needs. If one is sufficient, well and good. If more are desired at every time of sexual intimacy, then this should be prepared for and the necessary time taken to ensure that full satisfaction is obtained. The point that needs to be stressed here is that, as I have so frequently been suggesting, there should be the fullest consultation with each other about every phase of this subject. It is not enough to treat it lightly and to "see how things go." This is among the first duties of a wise and loving husband. He should ensure that everything is done to get for his wife the full satisfaction she craves, even if it means holding back from the sleep he is longing for. Careful thought will remove a host of roadblocks from the way.

How does pregnancy begin?

The sex organs of the woman are within the body. Two glands are situated deep in the pelvic area of the body, that is, in the region of the hips, and these glands are responsible for the manufacture of the female egg cells. The glands which act as such egg-forming organs are known as the ovaries. Between the ovaries is the uterus, or as it is better known, the womb. From each ovary to the uterus there is a connecting tube, known as the fallopian tube (the name is derived from the Italian anatomist who did extensive research on these tubes). The womb itself is one of the strongest and best defended parts of a woman's body. At its center there is a small cavity which is capable of tremendous extension while a baby grows within it. The lower end of the womb tapers to the cervix, and this fits into the top of the vagina. Inside the folds of the vagina is the urethra—much shorter in the female than in the male; and as we have already noted, in front above the entrance of the vagina is the clitoris. This we have seen to be one of the most central points of sexual feeling.

Ovaries produce, just as the testicles in the male, two materials. One is a hormone which is absorbed naturally into the bloodstream and produces those qualities characteristic of women:

enlargement of the breasts in puberty, a particular distribution of hair, as well as other female characteristics in personality and mind. The other material produced by the ovaries is the ovum or egg cell. One egg is released from an ovary approximately every twenty-eight days. This period of release is called the ovulation period. If pregnancy is to occur, a live egg cell must encounter a live sperm cell. The eggs are released from the ovaries into the fallopian tubes. Conception usually takes place in the fallopian tubes and the fertilized egg is moved gradually from the fallopian tubes to the womb. Here it is safely implanted on the wall of the uterus and begins to grow. The normal period for the development of a baby from conception to birth is nine months. Is it any wonder that Paul should say when writing to the church in Corinth: "Now the body is not one member but many. . . . God has harmonized the whole body by giving importance of function to the parts . . . that the body should work together as a whole with all its members in sympathetic relationship with one another" (I Corinthians 12:14, 24, 25 Phillips)?

Why does menstruation stop during pregnancy?

Menstruation occurs every twenty-eight days in all normal women. It is part of the cycle of life ordained by God for the preservation of the human race. On reaching physical maturity, every woman has built into her body the most elaborate mechanism for the development of children. When the egg cell is being developed, an additional amount of blood is supplied to the womb in order to strengthen it and in order also to nourish the egg cell should it be fertilized. If, however, the egg is not fertilized, there is no need for the womb to carry through its essential function. Accordingly, the increased lining of the uterus and the added supply of blood for the strengthening of the womb are expelled from the body through the vagina. But should pregnancy begin, should the egg cell be fertilized by the live sperm cell, then all that added strength is needed, is stored up, is put to use in order to establish the securest of homes for the developing foetus. Menstruation therefore ceases for the period of nine months during which the baby is growing in the womb of the mother.

The entire process of reproduction is part of the infinite wisdom of "God who only doeth wondrous things." The more one sees of the wonder of the body, its birth and growth, its uniqueness and marvels, the more one is brought to adore the Lord God. Praise is the only answer.

Can you say something about the hymen?

The word is Greek in origin. It means "covering" or "skin" or "membrane." The hymen is located at the portal of the vagina. It is a fold of mucous membrane which partially closes the vagina. It can vary in size and thickness; indeed, in some cases it does not break on the entrance of the penis, it merely stretches. A broken hymen does not always indicate lost virginity. Occasionally a girl is born without a hymen. Or the hymen may have been broken by strenuous exercise or by the insertion of a vaginal tampon to absorb the menstrual flow or during internal medical examination.

When the hymen is broken there may be some bleeding, slight or considerable according to the structure and strength of the membrane. This is perfectly normal. My own advice when talking to any group of young women on this subject is that they themselves break the hymen. It can save a great deal of discomfort at certain times; and in the normal course of events it is going to be broken anyway. Hard pressure by the index finger will settle the problem without difficulty. For centuries the hymen has been regarded as the inviolable sign of virginity, sentinel of the purity of maidenhood, true indicator of chastity. But such attention is out of all proportion to its function, which is *absolutely nothing.* It still is the case that a majority of men in our Western culture want to marry a virgin—and they may regard a broken hymen as a sign that the woman they have married has lost her virginity. This is a matter that the wife—or bride to be—should openly explain to the man of her choice.

Are there any other points on which we should be careful?

Well, it is always advisable to have read a great deal about the physiological and anatomical variations of male and female. You should know, as a husband, that your wife's body undergoes a cyclic ebb and flow that affects her body generally and her genitals in particular. The ovaries secrete and produce progesterone along with the ova or eggs, and they also produce an oestrogen of a similar type, which acts constantly. Many pharmaceutical firms today are manufacturing synthetic forms of oestrogen-progesterone, and these productions can very significantly extend or shorten the menstrual cycle. Such synthetic hormones can be of great help in correcting certain disorders and irregularities of menstruation. Ovulation can now be controlled by drugs to a certain extent, as we shall discuss further when we talk about birth control. But there are still great question marks over many things—there are a great number of things that the medical doctor still does not know. Why is the menstrual cycle twenty-eight days? Why does the ovary cease to function and go into retirement at a certain age? We may know much. But we do not know all.

I mention these things so that you come to one another with a deep appreciation of the complexity of one another's mortal bodies. It could be that you expect perfect performance every time you seek intercourse with one another. But the rhythmic cycle might not be working just right at that time. And you, the husband, may find that there is a certain time in each month when you have little or no desire to be joined in sexual intimacy; might almost feel as though you are joined to a stranger. Take these things in your stride. If you expect them to happen, you will not be surprised when they do. In any case, see to it that nothing separates you from one another.

Well, I don't think we're troubled on this score. Is there anything else?

You mustn't forget that there are certain types of mental illness that make marriage inadvisable. One must of course move with great delicacy here. I have known men and women who have spent many months in a mental clinic and for whom indeed we despaired of their ever getting better—but they did. And I have seen them married, living in the happiest of homes, with obviously well-balanced children around them. I recall one particular instance in which I felt that marriage was the last thing that the one-time mental patient should consider, and I said so. As a result of saying so, there came a total breakdown of communication and I heard nothing until news came of a wedding. I waited, still sceptical. But I was wrong. The cure was as complete as one could hope for and the resultant marriage has been most happy.

Much of course depends on the nature of the mental ailment. In this realm, modern psychiatry has made giant strides in the past twenty years. What was once counted impossible, is now a commonplace. New drugs, too, have been discovered which through their tranquilizing powers are able to hold in check the rise of feelings of hostility and alienation out of which so much of mental breakdown has come in the past. He is a wise man who will refuse to generalize in this field.

Nonetheless there are certain conditions of mental sickness that make marriage undesirable. If you have any doubt about your mental health, you should consult the best doctor in the field. If marriage is inadvisable, he will be able to detect that. If you need help and such help is available, he will be able to recommend a course of action.

What about epilepsy?

This to me is a fascinating question, because of the number of cases I have met and the peculiar friendship I have shared with some of them.

Epilepsy is a chronic disorder of cerebral function characterized by periodic seizures. Epileptic seizures are generally classified under four heads: (1) *grand mal,* in which incontinence, loss of consciousness, and an involuntary contraction of all the muscles of the body occur, causing the person to thrash about unconsciously for three or four minutes; (2) *petit mal,* in which occurs only a clouding of the consciousness for anything up to thirty seconds, but no falling; (3) *psychomotor,* in which there are confusion, staggering, and purposeless movements, but again with no falling; (4) *epileptic equivalents,* where the seizure may take the form of paroxysmal abdominal pain or mental cloudiness lasting for several hours. In about 75 per cent of these cases, no reason can be found for the disturbance. Treatment in general is nowadays through general sedatives to alleviate, restrain or prevent attacks.

What shall we say of this? I think we can be quite specific. If there has been no mental deterioration, and if in general the family history is good, there would appear to be no real grounds for denying marriage. But the best medical advice should be taken. A skilled doctor might determine that the condition could be aggravated by marriage, in which case he would probably counsel against it. On the other hand, when over an extended period of time there has been regular response to sedation and a course of drugs can be followed that seems to keep the condition in check, I would certainly advise marriage. I have known situations in which there has been the highest fulfillment.

What other kind of exceptional cases have you met?

I have a clergyman friend who works constantly among deaf and dumb people. He has told me of marrying handicapped couples from his congregation after satisfying himself on all the other conditions, and the results have been quite remarkable. Perfectly normal births have taken place, and the children have grown up to be a very wonderful help to their parents. In every case like this, one should satisfy himself that there is no legal impediment to the marriage and that for other basic reasons there is good evidence that the union will prove to be helpful and uplifting. Another of my friends in the ministry has also been working for a long time among physically handicapped people, and from time to time has been asked to marry a couple from their ranks. In almost every case, he tells me, he has agreed; and so far as he has been able to follow them up, there has been no occasion for regret. It so happens that in each of these cases there was a strong Christian faith to help them through whatever special problems arose. One can only say that God is able to make His grace to abound even in exceptional circumstances such as these, and can give years of joy to what would otherwise have been a grey and cheerless existence. Who could or would deny marriage under such circumstances?

I once married a couple in a hospital room when it was known for certain that the groom was going to die. This was a most solemn moment—full of joy, and yet our eyes were filled with tears as well. "For everything there is a season," says the writer of Ecclesiastes, "and a time for every purpose under heaven. A time to be born, and a time to die; a time to kill and a time to heal; a time to weep and a time to laugh." He concludes his soliloquy by adding: "God has made everything lovely in His time; also He hath set the world in their heart, so that man can find out the work that God maketh from beginning to the end." Bear all this in mind as you remember His mercies towards yourself. And "fear God and keep His commandments."

Is there anything else in this area we should know?

Possibly there is. I hesitate to speak of this, for I know it has no application in your own case. But it is worth knowing.

There is a very real possibility of syphilis and gonorrhea being transmitted by birth. We will study this later in the appropriate chapter. Any mother with active syphilis will almost certainly pass it on to her child. This is the kind of situation that has to be remembered when you read the second commandment and particularly that part of it which says: " . . . for I the Lord thy God am a jealous God, visiting the iniquity of the fathers upon the children unto the third and fourth generation." That is often criticized as a commandment totally lacking in love. But when you read further, you come to these words: " . . . and showing mercy unto thousands of them that love Me and keep My commandments." Jeremiah the prophet refers to an ancient saying in Israel—"The fathers have eaten a sour grape and the children's teeth are set on edge." That fact is unavoidable. Sin can never be kept to oneself. Someone else always suffers along with us. And in this tremendous realm of the life-process, if the wages of sin are known in one body, any other life proceeding from that body may likewise know the tragic toll of identical wages of grief. Gonorrhea exemplifies this equally well. At birth, a child passing through an infected birth canal may emerge with both eyes infected with the disease. Total or partial blindness may result from this. Medical skill if present can provide an antidote to the disease. But if such skill is not available, another poor life may be thrust out into the world with sightless eyes. It is good for you to know this. At some time you will meet with others who may need this kind of advice. See that you give it to them in the right way, with the right word and at the right time.

7: The Honeymoon

I've been wondering for a long time about what you would have to say on the subject of the honeymoon.

Well, this first. It will be one of your greatest blessings in life if as you grow in years you can look back on lingering memories of a joyous and ecstatic honeymoon.

A honeymoon is needed after the stress, the feverous rush of preparation, the last-minute thinking about details for the wedding. You need to get away by yourselves. You will have already been often in one another's company alone. But now there is a difference. You are not separated at the end of a happy evening. You continue together. And as you continue together, you have all the more opportunities for getting to know each other better, for learning to love one another more, and in general for adjusting your lives more completely to your alter egos.

Honeymoons are of course meant to be idyllic. They cannot last forever. You have to get back to work. Your vacation time is limited. But you must make the most of it while you can. This should be the first time that you sleep in the same bed together. That in itself is a great adventure. You are going to be in a new situation of undress with one another. That too can be exciting—very exciting. A honeymoon can become a time for the elimination of many fears and wonders that have been constant companions with you for many a year. All this is involved in these first joyous days of togetherness.

It is wise to settle where you spend your first night. Do remember that the wedding itself with the long reception will leave you exhausted. If, in addition to this, you add several hours' driving, you are certainly not going to be in any fit condition for the enjoyment of one another's company. It is really wise to try to get the wedding preparations all complete by three or four days before the wedding, and to try to get as much sleep as possible on these last nights at home. In this way, you will help ensure that your wedding night won't find you wearied.

Is it wise to seek sexual intimacy on that first night?

No! Not unless you feel so drawn to one another that nothing else will do. Intimacy between husband and wife is a great art, and it can easily be spoiled by inept and hasty action. I of course know of some couples who have felt it their "duty" to have their first sexual experience that night—and possibly you have heard of this too. But, for what it's worth, my advice is to take everything a little at a time. To sleep together—and sleep really shouldn't be too difficult if you are naturally tired—can be sufficient togetherness for that first night of joy.

In talking over experiences in marriage counselling sessions, I have found that many who went ahead with sex relations on their wedding night found them disappointing and frustrating. But there are exceptions to every rule and your case might well be the classic exception. If so, don't let anything deter you. So long as you are both agreed—with the kind of agreement of which we have already spoken much and will speak much more when we come to think about establishing a Christian home—then the way is open for you to do what you want. You are alone. You are alone in a sense in which you have never been before. You are now alone in that unique oneness which the minister has stated during the wedding service: "Wherefore they are no more twain, but one flesh." You are not two of you in that room. There is only one—in God's sight. You are one flesh. Do as He directs.

What do you suggest as the first thing a married couple should do on their honeymoon?

That's easy, though I may not give you the answer you expect. My very first act would be one of worship. Take your Bibles and read together a passage that you especially like—maybe a passage you have agreed on beforehand for reading together just then. You may want to read two different passages, one chosen by each of you. Good. Then kneel together and praise God for all His marvellous goodness to you. It is a tremendous day that you are looking back on. In your experience there has never been a day like it. Praise God for His goodness, His care of you, His wonderful provision of you to one another. Use simple but sincere words. There is no better prescription that I know for setting the right atmosphere and for preparing the way for whatever else is to come.

Laughter will fill your mind. There is seldom a wedding without lots of good, wholesome fun. Recall all you can. If telegrams have come to you, read them again. There may be verses of Scripture noted in the cables. Read the passages and underline them, marking the date on which you do so. This will be most valuable treasure in days ahead. You may want to dash off a note to your parents telling them that all is well. One thing is certain—they will be anxiously awaiting word from you. Keep them informed. Then, when everything has been done that you want or have to do, you are present for each other to possess as you feel best.

In most cases, it is natural for each to help undress the other. There are statistics on this gathered by a host of pollsters. But I'm not interested in pursuing this. All that needs be said is that an ingrained feeling of modesty is not lightly shed on one's first wedding night. For some it should be easy; each partner should decide what seems best and follow through accordingly. Keep the night sacred whatever you do.

Your wife may be in no hurry for anything more than sleeping together. Respect her wishes. Patience shown at a time like this will earn you love and devotion deeper than you will ever realize. In any case, about 90 per cent of all cases fail to achieve sexual success on the first attempt. Better leave this till later if you want to carry into the future a memory of your first honeymoon night as one completely beautiful, joyful and carefree.

I got a letter once from a couple whom I had just married. It was written the day after the wedding. This meant that the first night of their married life was behind them. They wrote:

> First of all a word of renewed thanks for yesterday. For us both it was a day of perfect bliss. The marriage ceremony we found deeply moving and, strangely enough, neither of us was in the least excited. The presence of all our friends,

the sense of being in our own home church and the whole atmosphere of joy made the service unforgettable.

Now, as you will see, we are on the Gulf of Mexico. The plane got in about 8 o'clock and by 9 we had reached the motel. It is right on the beach. It was dark of course by the time we arrived but we got to our room, unpacked, prayed together, and as neither of us was hungry—we had a huge meal on the plane, and that after the wedding meal—we went for a walk.

It is hard to describe what we felt. We were alone and that was a heaven in itself. We had the knowledge that for a whole two weeks we were going to be there—no rushing to work in the morning, nothing like that at all. Just rest. We walked along the beach and as we walked the moon rose—a full moon. Across the water of the waveless Gulf a silver path of light made its way to us wherever we walked. The night was warm and balmy and some of the scents of the flowering trees were heady and wild. I think we walked for nearly two hours, just talking about everything and praising God for His goodness. When we got back to the motel, we were both ready for sleep. And of course it was a sleep as we had never slept before—together! What a thrill to drift into slumber together. We shall never forget this day or night as long as we live.

That reads to me like a rather good beginning. It certainly was the prelude for what has proved to be a life of joyous and happy service for God.

May I raise a very practical point? How often—or do you know—does a honeymoon begin during menstruation?

About 17 per cent of all weddings occur while the woman is in menstruation. Naturally, most girls try to plan their wedding for a time when there will be no menstrual flow. But in spite of the best of planning, mistakes happen, and the percentage above is reasonably accurate.

What should be done in such cases? It is of course perfectly possible for sexual intimacy to occur during menstruation, but I would strongly advise against it at the beginning of married life.

My advice is to let the days go happily by until menstruation ceases. It is good for the wife to acquaint her husband with the nature of her own problems during the monthly period. These vary in a hundred ways and it is good to ensure that he is fully informed. There are cases, believe it or not, of men entering marriage without knowing what menstruation is and what pain it can cause.

There is no real loss if the honeymoon does begin during this period. It gives the couple all the longer time for self-adjustment and thereby to be more relaxed in each other's company as they approach their first experience in sexual intimacy. It is possible that a girl may be extremely self-conscious if her bridal day commences with the onset of her monthly period. But, as in all matters of life, be natural about it. There is really no reason in the world why this should not prove a very useful time.

What pitfalls may we expect during the honeymoon?

Well, you may have been taught to expect everything but the moon. From what you have heard from others you may well imagine that every day should be better than the day before and that everything should conspire to fill your days with joy.

It doesn't always work out that way. I recall my own honeymoon. It rained most of the time at the place where we had planned to stay, and eventually we decided to change our plans and we landed in London, England. It was the first time my wife and I had visited London together and the memory of these exciting days will never be erased. But you are still human—and so is the one to whom you are wedded. You may find on the third or fourth day a delayed reaction setting in and this must be watched carefully. Guard well each day.

Unconsciously, subconsciously or even consciously we all succumb to the glamour of the advertiser. The general theme is that happiness can be found by money or worldly success or sensual indulgence. Drugs and alcohol play a very important part in our generation and they are offered us in gorgeous technicolor or stereophonic sound. All this kind of advertising has given to the honeymoon an aura of gold that can be very deceiving. This is the spirit of the age. And among my first counsels to all going off on honeymoon is not to expect too much and to find more in each other than from any other source. Today, sex has been elevated into a cult. Eros has more worshippers among civilized men than any other god. To this there have been many contributing factors. Movies and television present a whole nation with sensuous women and amorous young men locked in passionate embrace. Shorter working hours and a profusion of time-saving gadgets have provided more leisure time for everyone. Add to all this the hundreds of wily advertising campaigns that use sex as a rather obvious bait to draw in buyers for all kinds of products and add along with them the degraded columnists who have given their lives to the task of publicizing empty nobodies with the faces of angels and the morals of an alley cat. Take all this along with those types of people who under the guise of literature peddle their overflow from the sewers of their souls to provide entertainment to the masses. This is the kind of world in which we live. And it is difficult to escape becoming ensnared.

This happened to Chester and Yvonne during their honeymoon. "You know how it is, pastor," Chester said to me. "We had this long evening before us. There wasn't much doing where we were, and we suddenly thought of visiting one of the movie shows. You know that in our homes we were told that there wasn't much worthwhile in such places and, by and large, except for what are known as the best of family movies, we had kept away from them. But Yvonne didn't demur when I suggested it, and we went. I want to tell you we felt awful. There was violence the like of which I hadn't believed possible, nudity right through, and free love advocated as a norm for the now generation. We left early, sick in mind and sad at heart. We both felt that we had got nothing from the night, that if we had planned the day more carefully we could have used the time far more profitably, and that the whole fetid mess had the smell of hell and death about it."

This is what I mean when I say you cannot be too careful. Places like these are no place for Christians. This is the kind of thing you should settle during your engagement days. To insert it as part of a honeymoon program is the nadir of folly.

Why is it that we see today such a mixup of moral values and concepts?

Well, you must never forget that the Bible has foretold that instead of becoming a better place the world is going to get worse and worse. As a matter of fact, the extraordinary situation that prevails in the realm of morals today ought to be taken as one of the greatest proofs of divine inspiration. All through the Bible there is a very strong emphasis both on marital fidelity and on pre-marital chastity. In the Christian tradition the essence of morality has to a greater rather than to a lesser degree appeared to consist of sexual restraint.

Now this has changed. In 1967 a television network in the United States offered a long documentary on the state of sexual morality among young people. Soon afterwards, the penetrating TV critic Harriet Van Horne stated that a number of the adult so-called experts who participated in the debate gave a very lackluster performance; then she added, "If they served no better purpose though, they provided a clue to what has induced the mild but unmistakable moral anarchy that pervades so many campuses today." She remarked that nowhere was there any sense of "a strong moral presence." There was literally "nobody who was prepared to say 'no.' " For almost a generation the professionals in family-life education, sex education and marriage counselling, as well as most of the authors of textbooks dealing with sex behavior, have been increasingly scientific disciples of sociology, psychology, psychiatry and anthropology. In areas such as these moral concepts are bothersome. For many who teach these sciences they simply don't belong in their field. And the result has been that increasingly the whole field has been taken over by amoral students of the whole subject. The Christian behaviorist has been notable for his absence.

This is all the more disastrous when you recall the figures who have dominated this field of study for so long. Sigmund Freud saw sexual instincts motivating so much of human activity—and that very particularly in his work among emotionally disturbed patients. One of his dominant conclusions was that a great measure of the world's neuroses was caused by repressed sexuality. It should be noted that in later years he modified many of his earlier findings and that it is possible to quote him in favor of sexual restraint—he himself was only slightly under the control of sexual drives and at the age of forty put an end to the physical aspect of his sex life. It goes without saying, however, that

Freud's writings and findings paved the way for a large measure of our twentieth-century permissiveness.

Alfred Kinsey likewise made a tremendous contribution in this direction, working under the Rockefeller Foundation and the University of Indiana and making extensive surveys of patterns of human sexual behavior. These were published as *Sexual Behavior of the Human Male*(1948) and *Sexual Behavior of the Human Female*(1953). As a biologist, he took a naturalistic view of sexual behavior, and this of course allied him with those who took a permissive stance. More recently, human sexual responses have been elaborately studied by William H. Masters and Virginia E. Johnson, whose research methods have shocked and startled millions of people while at the same time fascinating and attracting as many more. The point I'm making here is that all the greatest work in this area in the twentieth century has been performed by men without Christian conviction and that the results they have presented have in themselves proved sufficiently disturbing as to create an entirely new ethos and form of thought.

The result has been that our Western society has been abandoning its Judeo-Christian tradition as a basis for law and morality (and that of course includes sexual morality) without replacing it with anything comparable, without supplying any consistent alternative rationale for morality. And while this has been happening, extremely ingenious and effective means have been discovered to encourage a mood of hedonism. In the mid-1960s one of the fastest growing major magazines, *Playboy*, committed itself with complete dedication to upholding, applauding, commending and selling the hedonistic, sensual way of life. Hugh M. Hefner has written extensively on his philosophy. It hardly needs to be said that his position is a highly permissive one; and it is among the wonders of this day that clergymen have been found willing to debate in the pages of *Playboy* the rights and wrongs of pre-marital and extra-marital sex.

All these various forces have played a part in creating our modern tolerant and indulgent society. And tragically, along with the rise of these forces and philosophies, there has been an abdication by the Christian Church of the part she has historically played. Much of the blame for the present anarchy in morals must be laid at the door of the Church. For as the Church has lost her sense of being the custodian and trustee of the eternal truths of revelation, and as she has increasingly succumbed to the power plays of worldliness and materialism, she has had no right to demand that the ethic she herself is stubbornly refusing to follow in certain great areas of life should be followed by the rest of the world in those areas that deal with sex and procreation.

It may seem surprising to you that we should get involved in a question like this while we are really discussing the honeymoon of a Christian couple. But, and this cannot be too strongly urged, a Christian couple must settle quite definitely by what standards they are going to be ruled and how far, if at all, they are going to allow the general permissiveness that is all around in the very air they breathe to determine their actions and the way they will establish their home.

For this reason, I don't think this is out of place at all. A honeymoon is certainly a good place to discuss these issues exhaustively and to ensure that you are agreed together on their most important elements.

Does the Bible give any example of an ideal marriage?

You may be sure it does. You find it in the last chapter of the Book of Proverbs. There are thirty-one chapters in Proverbs, you know, just enough for one chapter for every day of the month. I know of no book that pays better dividends than the Book of Proverbs does. Read it to be wise and pursue its instructions if you would be godly. In the last chapter there is portrayed an idyllic scene—the perfect portrait of the perfect wife.

> Who can find a capable wife?
> Her worth is far beyond coral.
> Her husband's whole trust is in her,
> and children are not lacking.
> She repays him with good, not evil,
> all her life long.
> She chooses wool and flax
> and toils at her work.
> Like a ship laden with merchandise,
> She brings home food from afar.
> She rises while it is yet night
> and sets meat before her household.

After careful thought she buys a field
and plants a vineyard out of her earnings.
She sets about her duties with vigour
and braces herself for the work.
She sees that her business goes well,
and never puts out her lamp at night.
She holds the distaff in her hand,
and her fingers grasp the spindle.
She is openhanded to the wretched
and generous to the poor.
She has no fear for her household when it snows,
for they are wrapped in two cloaks.
She makes her own coverings,
and clothing of fine linen and purple.
Her husband is well known in the city gate
when he takes his seat with the elders of the land.
She weaves linen and sells it,
and supplies merchants with their sashes.
She is clothed in dignity and in power
and can afford to laugh at tomorrow.
When she opens her mouth, it is to speak wisely,
and loyalty is the theme of all her teaching.
She keeps her eyes on the doings of her household
and does not eat the bread of idleness.
Her sons with one accord call her happy;
her husband too and he sings her praises:
"Many a woman shows how capable she is;
but you excel them all."

Is there one item of advice more than any other that you give to honeymooners—if they ask for it?

There certainly is. I learned this lesson many years ago and its importance I cannot exaggerate.

Let me state it very simply. A true honeymoon should find you beginning to act constructively as a couple. We are all individualists by nature, whether we be extroverts or introverts. But marriage and the marriage bed is no place for asserting your rugged individualism. Your first essays at sexual intimacy should always be essays in togetherness. To act constructively as a couple means that you will deliberately refuse to assert yourself or to display your special gifts or powers. If your first attempts at sexual intimacy end in failure, you mustn't blame the other. After all, even Dr. Kinsey's massive studies demonstrate that the best-matched couples regard achieving orgasm on about two-fifths of sexual occasions as par. It is very seldom that you will achieve mutual synchronization of orgasm. Time and experience may show you the best way for yourselves. But whatever you do, be sure that you do it together—as a couple. Otherwise, you may find that you are blaming yourself for some unknown but suspected sexual inadequacy, and the resulting loss of confidence may compound your problem. If on the other hand you blame your partner, that too will take its toll in friction and tension and a thousand nameless fears. Act as a couple. Experiment as a couple. Grow as a couple.

It goes without saying that honeymooners have had their minds filled with a host of fancies about the delights that await them. But a lot of this is nonsense and ballyhoo. Joy there will be; and true delight. Thank God for that! But there will be times in the first few weeks when you feel upset and restrained. At times like these, help one another. As you do, God will show His perfect way.

During our honeymoon, should we concentrate more on things mental than things physical?

Well, that is a hard question to answer. I certainly don't think much of a honeymoon that is taken up entirely with physical and sexual exploration. You must see to it that as you begin to operate as a couple and not as individuals you really concentrate on bringing your thinking into the same level and that you pattern your thoughts as much as possible after each other's. But a honeymoon is a step-by-step program. You cannot separate yourself from the pleasure of physical contact. You have looked forward with anticipation to the day when you will be wholly free to share yourselves with one another. That means the sharing of your body with your life-partner; and that can be a very wonderful experience. John Milton wrote for all the human race when he pictured Eve responding to Adam in Book IV of *Paradise Lost.*

> "With that thy gentle hand
> Seized mine: I yielded, and from that time see
> How beauty is excelled by manly grace
> And wisdom, which alone is truly fair."
>
> So spake our general mother, and with eyes
> Of conjugal attraction unreproved,
> And meek surrender, half-embracing leaned
> On our first father; half her swelling breast
> Naked met his, under the flowing gold
> Of her loose tresses hid. He, in delight
> Both of her beauty and submissive charms,
> Smiled with superior love, as Jupiter
> On Juno smiles when he impregns the clouds
> That shed May flowers, and pressed her matron lips
> With kisses pure.

For Milton, the physical could not be separated from the contemplation of "manly grace and wisdom, which alone is truly fair." And yet, in words of great beauty, he writes of the pure joy of their physical union.

If during your honeymoon you are able to share full sexual intimacy with one another, you should certainly thank God for this. This fulness of union has been ordained of God for the perfecting of the marriage bond and for the drawing of both of you closer to one another, heart to heart and mind to mind. It is the considered judgment of most marriage counsellors that there is no need for husband and wife to have simultaneous orgasms. It is equally their judgment that marriage without both husband and wife enjoying orgasm is no true fulfillment. Your honeymoon may well be the time to think all these things through carefully and well. It may not be the time in which you have true success in attaining fulfillment. Never mind. That will come if you act cooperatively and consider one another's needs and help one another in this most sacred bond of union. The goal of all true life is to live according to the perfect will of God. It was of that we talked at the very beginning when we emphasized that every man's life is a plan of God and that God has His chosen one just for you. The same God created the processes through which full fulfillment of bodily needs can be met; and these needs, desires, processes and methods are all morally good when they are permitted to operate according to the plan of the Creator within the bond of the marriage union. Don't overestimate the place of the physical in your honeymoon days. Alternatively, don't undervalue the ties that bind you as one in will, affection and thought.

Perhaps we could do no better than re-read the lovely lines of the Song of Songs, chapter 6, verses 1-10. Whatever interpretation is given ultimately to this book, it certainly is in the beginning a selection of very beautiful poems exalting the love relationships between husband and wife, praising and extolling the fidelity of married lovers, and describing with typical oriental simplicity and originality the physical joys and the spiritual blessedness of wedlock. Read in this way, the whole book is a fragrant commentary on the intimacy of the marriage bond. And if in its full expression marriage is a foreshadowing of the heavenly union of Christ with His Church, there should be no hesitation in allowing Christian imagination to follow this through to the love which Christ has for His Church and His infinitely strong compassion that embraces her. Here is the passage I've just mentioned:

Companions:

Where has your beloved gone,
O fairest of women?
Which way did your beloved go,
that we may help you to seek him?

Bride:

My beloved has gone down to his garden,
to the beds where balsam grows,
to delight in the garden and to pick the lilies.
I am my beloved's, and my beloved is mine,
he who delights in the lilies.

Bridegroom:

You are beautiful, my dearest, as Tirzah,
lovely as Jerusalem.
Turn your eyes away from me,
they dazzle me.

Your hair is like a flock of goats streaming down from Mount Gilead; your teeth are like a flock of ewes come up fresh from the dipping, each ewe has twins, and none has cast a lamb.

Your parted lips behind your veil
Are like a pomegranate cut open.

There may be sixty princesses,
eighty concubines, and young women past counting,
but there is one alone, my dove, my perfect one,
her mother's only child,
devoted to the mother who bore her;
young girls see her and call her happy,
princesses and concubines praise her.
Who is this that looks like the dawn,
Beautiful as the moon, bright as the sun,
majestic as the starry heavens?

All God's creative planning has gone into this creation of marriage where "a man shall leave his father and mother and shall be joined to his wife." How beautifully it is put again in the Song of Songs (2:6): " . . . his left arm was under my head, his right arm was round me." Could anything more aptly describe the feelings, dreams, romanticisms, spiritual and sexual joys of true lovers? Mental and physical are one. Truth and beauty are one. Man and woman are one. This is God's plan. See that you keep it unsullied and pure.

8: Impotence and Frigidity

What is impotence?

The inability of a man to complete coitus with a woman. This can take various forms and the result in every case is utter frustration. Nonconsummation of marriage through failure to complete intercourse can become a cause for divorce. You can understand, therefore, how a man begins to feel who loves his wife but finds himself unable at the crucial moment to give her the sexual intimacy that is hers by right. A frustrated donor and a disillusioned recipient are both victims of sexual torture. At times, it would be an absolute impossibility to say who suffered the most.

Jessica was such a girl. She was married on a Saturday afternoon and they checked into a motel room about nine that night. For months she had been looking forward to this evening. But things didn't work out as she had hoped. It wasn't that Fred wasn't willing. He did everything in his power to satisfy her. But penile erection eluded him. By three in the morning, after exhausting themselves completely and finding that everything they attempted only added to the frustration and bafflement, they fell asleep. But after about two hours of sleep, Jessica awoke, grasped her suitcase after dressing while Fred slept on, and slipped out into the early morning.

I saw her that afternoon. Nothing that I could do would make her rethink her position. She felt herself tricked, beaten and defeated. The entire episode had turned into a nightmare and nothing could alter her stance.

"This is no marriage." She said it and she felt it. She would have nothing more to do with it. And the inevitable happened. She obtained a divorce on grounds of nonconsummation.

Is this kind of impotence a common thing?

No! But this "no" must be qualified. The design of the male sexual equipment is such that erection always subsides after ejaculation. This is a most valuable circuit breaker in the man's sexual mechanism, allowing time for the reproductive organs to function properly again. Normally, it takes anything from thirty minutes to a full hour for full power to be restored. During this period, the man is essentially impotent. It is absolutely crucial for his wife to realize this, for if by some mischance there has been on his part a loss of sperm through premature ejaculation, then there is just no way that his wife can enjoy complete sexual intimacy. Every wife should know this and be infinitely patient and understanding.

On the other hand, men should understand themselves fully. The delicately articulated structures of our genitals are controlled by highly tuned mechanisms concerned far more with quality than with quantity. Yet many men think they can drive themselves to a level of potency for which nature never endowed them. The result of this can be a failure to fulfill their highest hopes; and the end of this experience can be tragic and upsetting. The fact is that some men are seriously bothered by certain things and are turned off. The crying of a child in the room next door, the memory of some particularly upsetting episode at business during the day, a feeling of possible failure because of failure before—these are the kind of things that can make a man suddenly face the fact of impotency just at the moment when he wants to be the strongest and most virile of men. Virility is often affected by some chance thought, some random fear, some uncertainty about almost anything. Impotence can become extremely baffling and annoying to both partners, and it is a wise man who will discuss this possibility with his bride.

Are there various forms of impotence?

Yes! And one of them really poses under the guise of hyperpotency. I have already referred to it. It occurs in cases where penile erection is easy and speedy, and the moment the male makes contact with his counterpart, ejaculation occurs. This condition is medically known as premature ejaculation. This may take an infinite variety of forms, but they all have one thing in common—there is no possibility of satisfying the female. Most women who are at the receiving end of this treatment feel there must be a basic abnormality in their mates. They feel cheated, defrauded, victimized. And who can blame them? Yet men who suffer from this are equally unhappy about it. It always happens involuntarily. Given time, it may be overcome. But it can be self-defeating in countless ways. It certainly takes a very forbearing woman to tolerate this for long.

At the other end of the scale there is what is known as psychogenic aspermia. In this case the very opposite to what we have been discussing occurs. Everything in the man's sexual performance is perfect and without error. All that is wrong is that the man never ejaculates. It is the male equivalent, if you like, of female frigidity, about which we'll presently talk. This man suffering from what may be euphemistically called "P.A." can never complete the sexual act. There is always a basic mental reason for this. It is one of the conditions which any psychiatrist who knows the rudiments of his work can help very speedily. In fact, normal sexual functioning can be made to occur rapidly if the right help is found. Great care, however, should be taken. There is always the possibility of permanent damage being done to the personality through circumstances such as these. Once again, the advantage of being on the best of terms with a good doctor is self-evident. At times like these he should be sought out speedily.

Are there other reasons for such impotence?

Yes. I have already said that there is always a mental block in cases of psychogenic aspermia. You may be ruled in your memory by something that is distinctly unpleasant in its sexual associations. Such memories may go far back in time. It may be that you were the object of attack by a sexual pervert at a very susceptible age. This can carry over into maturity. Problems like this can and should be treated by skilled psychoanalysis. Otherwise, you may carry on with your troubles and be, in Churchill's great phrase, "decided only to be undecided, resolved to be irresolute, adamant for drift, solid for fluidity, all-powerful to be impotent."

Should your emotional relationships in maturity develop from models that date back to childhood, sexual impotence can easily develop. Your first attraction to your wife may be from some resemblance to your mother or sister; and some trace of this origin may remain even when the full transference has taken place. Yet, because sexual advances to the original figure would have been wrong, some of this sense of wrongness may remain in the case of the person to whom you have transferred your affections. A sense of guilt can grow. Thoughts of incest may intervene between you and your life-partner. Thereby real trouble may develop, and great care should be taken in treating any such cases.

In cases such as these, I always advise consultation with an expert in that field. In any first-class marriage counselling course there will always be several good doctors available; one of them should be a psychiatrist of proven worth. Trust him completely. Tell him the whole story. It will surprise you how much you can be helped together when as a *couple* you share your problems with him.

A friend recently said to me that a Christian shouldn't be troubled with problems like this, and he doubted the advisability of ever calling in the help of a psychiatrist. What do you say to this?

This first of all. Your friend is wrong. You might as well say that a Christian should never suffer from appendicitis or cancer or a sore back. But the fact is that Christians in all walks of life do suffer ailments and sicknesses which require skilled help, trained help, God-given help.

In the same way, you run into problems like this in scores of Christian homes. As a matter of fact, I shudder at times to think of the ignorance that exists in the cases of children reared in the relative insulation of a Christian home. I have known instance after instance of a young bride and groom coming to me for some marriage counselling prior to their wedding not knowing even the basic facts of life. Obviously, the parents have failed here. And if this is the case in matters of general anatomy, what must the situation be in areas where there are really deep problems?

As a minister, I am dealing all the time with people who are preparing for marriage; and I am also dealing with people who have been married for a long time but have obviously not known the way to tackle the problems that arise in any normal marriage.

One can only go so far in certain cases. A minister who has kept himself abreast of modern knowledge will readily recognize many of the obvious things. He will also know when it is possible for him to step in and help. At the same time, if he is a wise man, he will know where the dividing line falls between what are purely spiritual problems and what are cases for the mental clinic. This is sometimes one of the hardest things to learn. But anyone who wants to be of assistance must learn it. What I would have done without the help of some highly skilled psychiatrists during my ministry I just do not know.

At the same time, the reverse is the case. I recall once being called to visit a friend who was in deep trouble and whom nothing seemed to help. She had been to the best psychiatrists in town—to no avail! I came therefore into the situation fully warned that others had tried and failed. Very gingerly I took the first steps, probing a little here and a little there; and very soon I became persuaded that the basic problem was not neurotic, not nervous, not indeed anything that could be catalogued in the normal lists of ailments that a psychiatrist deals with. To me it seemed a clear case of spiritual neglect of the means of grace with a consequent sense of arrested development and a corresponding feeling of intense guilt. Once I was sure of this, I opened the Bible to the great passages of Scripture that tell of a pardoning God and of the richness of His promises to His children. One of them in particular we stayed with for a while: "I will restore to you the years that the locusts have eaten" (Joel 2:23). Well, one could make a long story out of it; but there is no need. The result was dramatic. From lying in bed for more than a month, getting up only for some group therapy sessions which were supposed to help, she was released almost instantaneously from her trouble and within a few days was at work very much her normal self.

What about frigidity in women? Is this common?

The word "frigidity" is used to denote any kind of impairment of sexual feelings in women. It covers a whole spectrum of sexual response and is frequently used to describe what is merely a substandard response to the appeal for sexual intimacy. It can mean anything from total avoidance of any sexual contact whatsoever, or any desire for it, to an occasional bypassed orgasm.

Is it common? It depends on many things and of course on what you regard as normality. It is probably more frequent in women than in men. But the word "frigidity" is itself a problematical word. There may be some fundamental organic weakness. Frigid means cold, and to use such a term in reference to a woman may well mean that she is sexually rejecting. Yet that may not be the case at all. This is an area in which I would counsel you to walk very guardedly and to choose your words with the greatest care.

Can you define some of the better-known symptoms?

Well, I can try. Like impotence in man, frigidity can range right across the board from total and obvious sexual failure to much more subtle manifestations. There may be real orgasmic impairment arising from very deep emotional problems. It is a well-established fact that every woman suffering from this kind of orgasmic impairment was reared in a home where there was no true love. In childhood, there was coldness and calculated cruelty at times; and this cuts deep into the personality of any girl. Adult behavior is sometimes a means of continuing or perpetuating the isolation and loneliness suffered as children. Our emotional problems pierce and permeate every aspect and phase of life—and this hold especially true in our sexual life. It is really very natural, therefore, for a woman who knew the hardness and coldness in youth of which we have been speaking to demonstrate much of this when she reaches a point where she is within reach of the deepest intimacy that two people can possibly have on earth. I recall vividly a case in point.

Michelle came from a home where there were only her sister and father besides herself. When I came to know her, the father had died and she was working on computers. She had few friends—none in point of fact. She had no enemies either; she was just a plain girl doing the rounds of duty and doing them very skillfully, for she was most capable. She dressed frowsily. She looked years older than she was. And one day her sister called me on the phone.

"I wish you could do something for Michelle. She seems to be losing all interest even in living. I should tell you that when she was much younger our Dad made her almost a slave. It was always 'Do this' or 'Do that.' She had always to be around. Neither of us can remember our mother; and Dad knew he couldn't do with me what he did with Michelle. I know also for a fact that from time to time he got her to sleep with him and you can guess what he was asking that for. Can't you do something? Since Dad died, she has gotten worse rather than better, and there seems to be something lurking deep beneath that bodes no good."

Well, Michelle and I met. At once I suggested that she consult a friend of mine who was chief psychiatrist in a nearby clinic. Very reluctantly she went, and was admitted for treatment with the basic problems of guilt, anxiety and depression. It took a long time for her to learn that she was subconsciously reproducing the bitterness, the numbness, the coldness and the loneliness of her childhood in her adult life. But slowly she discovered herself. It was like a new person being born. When she first began to receive treatment, she evinced no interest in sex. But that was just a cover-up, though gradually her problem was emaciating the whole area of sexual desire, and if treatment hadn't been found she would certainly have ended up a bitter and disillusioned old woman. Instead, the very opposite happened. Now she is married and has three of the loveliest children you have seen.

Here the answer to frigidity, which had reached proportions of the utmost seriousness, was psychotherapy. And there was no other answer. Deep emotional malfunction can most frequently manifest itself in sexual disinterest.

What other causes contribute to this condition?

Fear—most of all. Failure to reach orgasm is often a basic factor in inducing frigidity. It seems to work like this. Let a woman fail to reach an orgasm by the end of her honeymoon, and you may find her wondering if there is something basically wrong with the mechanism of her sexual nature. From that day on, anxiety tinges every sexual incident. Exaggerated expectations can often induce undue concern. All too often these great expectations simmer down to a mild sense of pleasure that she has been able to help her husband to find pleasure. But that is far from the ideal.

Much of this kind of fear can be very irrational. Many women fear injury during coitus. In preparation for intercourse, many women find themselves suffering waves of fear as they insert a diaphragm or carry out other birth-control procedures. The all-prevailing fear of cancer developing from some of the irritation created by a birth-control device can also be terrifyingly real. It is possible to dismiss this lightly. But when a woman has once become obsessed with a fear of this sort, it is not easy to remove.

There is a sense in which much of this fear is the product of an incomplete or a wrong upbringing. And it is at this point that we should affirm the great Christian freedoms which are the birthright of every true Christian. Every Christian home should be one where true concern and love are shown for each member of the family. And every Christian adult should accept fully and joyfully the freedom given in Christ to be all that he has intended us to be. "Fear has torment," writes the Apostle John, "but perfect love casts out all fear" (I John 4:18). Fear in itself is a perfectly healthy instinct. It is through fear that the human race has survived. But when fear becomes anxiety, worry, apprehension, nervousness, restlessness, tremor or heart-sinking, then the instinct has developed beyond its legitimate bounds and the time has come for treatment. I recall the words of Amelia Earhart Putnam:

> Courage is the price that life exacts for granting peace.
> The soul that knows it not, knows no release
> From little things;
> Knows not the livid loneliness of fear,
> Nor mountain heights where bitter joy can hear
> The sound of wings.

Too many know and live with "the livid loneliness of fear." But for the Christian this should not be. The heart of the message of the good news is that deliverance from fear is possible—from every kind of phobia and mistrust, from despondency and despair. And at this point, where we are thinking of frigidity in women that is caused and perpetuated by fear, it is so essential to continue repeating the words of everlasting hope that trumpet from the everlasting Scriptures. In the presence of Christ there is no need for fear. To rest in Him is the ultimate answer to all despair.

Does fear of pregnancy create frigidity?

Very often. Every woman has some natural aversion to pregnancy. The words of Genesis 3:16 have been fulfilled in countless women since first they were uttered: "I will greatly multiply thy sorrow and thy conception; in sorrow thou wilt bring forth children." Even where there is an overwhelming desire to be a mother, aversion to pregnancy as such is basic. If such fear becomes in any way irrational, then drag the whole subject out into the open and talk it over fully and freely with your husband. Here is another of the great areas where you must act as a couple and not as pure individuals. Pregnancy does involve major alterations in life patterns and many discomforts and physical disabilities. It is a time when you may not appear personally to the best advantage, and it eventually means breaks in sexual intimacy with your husband. All these considerations are very much in the mind of any girl who thinks at all, and this is a very natural thing. In his book *The Marriage Art* (one of the best books I know for describing the "how to" of marriage), Dr. John E. Eichenlaub says the following about the fear of pregnancy:

> Concern about the possibility of pregnancy is as normal to a married woman as fear of bullets to a soldier in battle. A wife doesn't have to deny her fear or rid herself of it in order to enjoy sex or undertake motherhood. Like the soldier, she usually does better by acknowledging her fear and letting other emotions, desires and loyalties overwhelm it. In this way she can take whatever actions are logical to quell her dread, mobilize emotional support and help which denial would not permit, and bring her feelings into proper proportion through the action of her own good sense and knowledge.

Any myth of one's own power turns him away from an honest recognition of his weakness and robs him of the strength of faith in God. But a true trust in God will break through every vicious circle of fear and the ills that follow it.

Are there different kinds of frigidity?

Yes. Much depends on what the woman is really trying to say. Subconsciously she chooses various methods of expressing herself, and this is one of the methods. There is a condition known as "vaginismus" in which the muscles of the vagina contract on the penis or against the penis. This convulsive or spastic contraction usually stems from fear, and this fear can be of many kinds—fear of pain, fear of intercourse itself, fear of pregnancy. Some of these fears may be so deeply rooted that only psychoanalysis could reveal them. When there is fear present, and when this condition persists, medical help should be sought. It may well be that the real need will be for psychiatric help. Don't be dismayed about this if it should happen to you. It is not an altogether unusual occurrence, and what is needed is to let the fresh winds of truth begin to play through your mind. Yet, it is never easy to assess accurately what a woman is trying to say when vaginismus appears. It may be perfectly involuntary. On the other hand, there may be some subterranean areas of guilt that are asserting themselves at the moment of coitus. Be wise. Consult the best advice you can get. It will almost certainly help.

There may be some infection of the vagina that should be attended to. See to this. Treatment should settle this easily. On the other hand, difficulty in copulation may result from some malformation of the genitals either of the man or woman. Such difficulty, and the anticipation of difficulty, can well cause frigidity. Difficulty in copulation may occur, especially in later life, from a deficiency of estrogenic hormones during the menopause. But only about 10 per cent of cases of vaginismus have a physical basis. The other 90 per cent of women who find intercourse painful or distasteful are in reality saying with their vagina what they would not wish to say with their tongue.

What kind of sexual sensations does the frigid wife feel?

None at all, really. She becomes inert. She is prepared to offer her body for her husband to use, but she refuses to become involved in any way. Loss of sexual feelings for one's husband can become a tremendous barrier to other types of communication. Indeed, it can be difficult sometimes to say which has come first—the breakdown of mental communication or the refusal to participate actively in sexual experiences. Any woman, given the necessary grounds for her action, can become prone and insensible during a period of intercourse.

Sexual anesthesia, as we might well call this, is far more widely spread than you might think. But it is a travesty of the good and perfect plan that God meant for man and wife. When God invented and created sex, He gave man one of the greatest gifts He could possibly grant him. As we have already said, He shared something of His own being with man when this gift was freely bestowed. And since it is given to draw husband and wife into ever deepening fellowship, love and support, the loss of it by either partner is a major calamity. In all fully Christian marriages, there should be the full enjoyment of sex as God gave it and as He meant it to be enjoyed. To deny it, is to deny a gift that has capacities of untold good for ourselves, our home and our whole circle of friends. Some women think of frigidity as a type of self-denial, and since self-denial is of the very essence of Christianity, then their frigidity should be all right. Not so! God's gifts are given to be enjoyed to the full.

Can frigidity be cured? How?

The best cure is prevention. Knowledge is always the key that unlocks the best of life's secrets and values; and given the right kind of knowledge through wise and capable training in early years, there should be no problem. Good, straightforward and absolutely honest education is the greatest step. To rob any child of the right kind of knowledge at the appropriate stages of development is to wrong that child in a most crucial way. Sex is universal. It is normal. It is human. And in addition, as I have repeatedly said, it is divine. Why then should there be any hesitation to tell a child the full story of sex as it is? The facts will vary with the age, but they will never conflict with one another. The right kind of sex education is a must in any true program of education. But the best place to begin is in the home. The best of all teachers in the beginning is the mother. She can initiate the children whom she has borne into the sacred mysteries of this holy gift of sex; and if she fails to do so, she is failing them at one of the most needy areas of their personality. The innate curiosity of the child will accept the wonder of conception and birth and, if truly spoken, there will never be any need to alter one single word in after years.

Above all else, one must say that frigidity, apart from physical causes, is really impossible where there is true love. Love will open every door of life. A couple joined in love will always attract one another. "There is no fear in love." We might well add, "There is no frigidity in love." Let love, then, rule and direct at every step of the way. Let the love of God be your pattern. When this is so, you may be sure all else is well.

9: The First Child

Tell us something about conception and birth.

Well, that is certainly a tall order. But it is good to know all the facts about how life commences and what takes place when a baby is born.

We are of course tremendously blessed in the Western world with so many skilled doctors who have made this their special study. They are called obstetricians or gynecologists. When once you know that a baby is likely to be born into your home, your first responsibility is to obtain the best of medical help and place yourself unreservedly in his hands.

There is no need for us to go over what we have already noted in the chapter on the anatomy and physiology of sex. We noted there how pregnancy begins and marked some of the wonderful details of human reproduction. Well, here you are looking forward to the coming of your first baby. At times, you are happy and excited; at other times, you are rather terrified at the thought. If you are like any other normal girl, you will have begun to read lots of articles in the newspapers and the magazines. At times, you may feel that the whole affair is going to be an extremely complicated kind of business. But it isn't really. Wait and see!

One thing is certain. You will get lots of advice from your friends who are mothers already. And if your own mother is still alive, she will be as excited as you are personally. She too will have lots of things to say. But don't let all you hear overawe you. You will find that you will adapt to the situation when the time comes and that everything will be just right. It is the considered judgment of all good doctors that what you and your husband naturally feel like doing is in actual fact best for the child. You can trust your instincts a great deal. Far better to make a few mistakes by being your own natural selves than to be letter-perfect but full of anxiety and worry.

Give us a good Bible passage to think about during days of pregnancy.

Well now, there are a hundred passages and more to which you could turn. But why not choose Psalm 127? Here it is.

> Except the Lord build the house, they labour in vain that build it. Except the Lord keep the city, the watchman waketh but in vain.
>
> It is vain for you to rise up early, to sit up late, to eat the bread of sorrows: for so He giveth His beloved sleep.
>
> Lo, children are a heritage of the Lord: and the fruit of the womb is His reward.
>
> As arrows are in the hand of a mighty man: so are children of the youth.
>
> Happy is the man that hath his quiver full of them: they shall not be ashamed, but they shall speak with the enemies in the gate.

I don't think you could get anything better than that. Houses are safe only when God protects them. Homes are established only through His blessing and grace. Let me quote again from Matthew Henry's comments on this passage:

> Those that desire children as an heritage from the Lord must receive them in the way that He is pleased to give, by lawful marriage to one wife. Children are indeed a heritage and a reward, and are so to be accounted, blessings and not burdens, for He that sends mouths will send meat to fill them if we trust in Him.

You may already be reflecting on the fact that the coming of the baby is going to be highly restrictive on the freedom you enjoy. As Dr. Spock writes in *Problems of Parents,* "When the first baby comes, the escape hatch seems to bang shut for an indefinite period. In motherhood there is no quitting. Vacations are not usually vacations at all. There is no salary. There are no promotions. The mothers with the most children have, on the average, the least time off, the fewest luxuries, the rarest distractions." All true! And it's at those times, when you think of the possible loss of freedom and the burdens that are going to be yours without fail, that you should take parts of the Bible like the one I've just mentioned and pray that your children will indeed prove to be "an heritage from the Lord." Behind the lives of many of God's choicest servants you can see so clearly the figure of a praying mother. Praying mothers make great men.

Would you say that the basic urge to have children is selfish or unselfish?

I have no hesitation in saying that you cannot separate one's own wishes from an irresistible instinct to share in parenthood. After all, if any parent sat down and counted the cost in hard work and deprivation, as well as the cost of providing for the children for something like twenty years, would any of them really plan on having a family? The fact is that any child who has been brought up in a reasonably satisfactory home, having known something of the love of parents who have tried to do their best, wants to become a loving parent more than anything else. The child imitates the mother from earliest years and goes on doing so far more than is realized. So I really think it's impossible to talk about things selfish or unselfish in this connection. It is a basic urge within the breast of any normal man or woman. Otherwise, there would never be real marriages and there would be no desire for children.

At the very heart of the creation ordinance God gave a commandment: "Be fruitful and multiply and replenish the earth" (Genesis 1:28). Man is therefore constituted in this way. There is no way in which he can escape his destiny. While the earth remains, the urge to marry, to have children and to repopulate the earth will abide. Every generation will find it as strong an urge as did the one before; and all the talk about birth-control plans and all world efforts to control population explosions are doomed to fail because man is what he is and woman is what she has always been.

How can a husband and wife best prepare for the coming of their child?

How can one answer a question like that adequately? So much is involved. There should certainly be on the husband's part even greater tenderness and solicitude for his wife than he has ever known or shown. That goes without saying. In the first five months of pregnancy there need be no undue alteration of your schedule; but during the last three months, and most particularly the last few weeks, it begins to seem as though the day will never come. You wish labor would begin even though you shrink from it. You are uncomfortable in a chair or even in bed. And all sorts of questions are in your mind: What will the baby be—boy or girl? Good or fussy? Healthy or—perish the thought—deformed? Every woman thinks thoughts such as these. Those who have lived through the agonizing years of the thalidomide babies and seen the grotesque malformations of body with which they must go through life to the very end cannot fail to wonder and pray that all will be well.

At times like these, husband and wife should learn a deeper reliance on one another. This is one of the great reasons why it is generally best to wait beyond your teens to marry. It is uncommon to find a teenage boy with the maturity and reserves on which to draw to support and strengthen his wife at a time like this. I always counsel that you be together as much as possible. Let the husband cut down on all unnecessary trips and stay around the house as much as possible. Share lovely things together. One of the most wonderful men I ever knew was an African who studied medicine in Edinburgh and returned to his native land to practice it. I watched him through the period when the first baby was coming. He surrounded his wife with lovely music. He read to her when he was free to do so. He showed her love in the simplest but loveliest ways. They prayed together, for they were both dedicated Christians. And when the baby came, the first thing they did was to dedicate that child to their God and Saviour.

What do you advise when the child is mongoloid?

Mongolism is the name given to a very special type of organic mental deficiency. It is a disturbance of bodily as well as mental development. The eyes slant upwards; growth is slow; intelligence develops very, very slowly and there are times when there is really no mental growth at all. Sometimes intelligence does develop to a fair degree, and as these children are usually sweet-natured, there is a real possibility of integration into a family circle.

Nonetheless it is a very vexing matter—one that I have met with occasionally. My wife and I were once asked to care for a little mongoloid girl for part of a summer vacation, along with her nurse. It was for our family a precious time, and we recall these days spent together with something of a sad nostalgia. In another case, where the level of intelligence was practically nil, we felt only embarrassment and pain in her presence.

I think that in cases such as these the parents must be fully agreed as to what to do. The worst thing that can happen is for one parent to wish the child placed in a home for such children while the other is determined to keep the child at home. Agreement is absolutely essential. Occasionally, this condition can be diagnosed at birth; but in a good number of cases it is not recognizable until the child is a few months old. Probably it is best to await signs of development. If there are other children in the home, their welfare must be considered too. A man told me not so long ago that his whole life had been seared by being raised alongside a brother with this condition. In most parts of the Western world there are now good state or private boarding establishments where the best medical and psychological attention can be given.

Do you ever advise adoption?

Frequently. But if adoption is to succeed, the parents must be fully agreed about it. The decision to adopt is often taken after several years of childless marriage, and the question is then discussed from every angle. Sometimes a wife who feels she is losing the affection of her husband will urge they adopt a child. This is not good. It is bad both for the child and for the prospective parents. Neither will gain, for all too often a child so adopted, sensing that he is not really loved, may prove extremely difficult.

But adoption has brought hope and joy to countless homes, as well as providing a home for a child who otherwise would face the darkest of futures. Undoubtedly there are today on this continent many babies without the security of a home of their own, and it should not be too difficult for a married couple who wish a child to find one and to bring that one up "in the fear, the nurture, and the admonition of the Lord." This has succeeded in countless cases. I think of the anonymous little poem:

Not flesh of my flesh,
Not bone of my bone,
But still most miraculously
All our own.

Never forget
For a single minute,
You didn't grow under my heart,
But in it.

Last summer I met in Oregon a couple who had two lovely Korean children with them, a boy and a girl, aged seven and eight years. I asked them if they had any family of their own, and they answered Yes. "But our own two girls are now married; and one day my wife and I sat and looked at each other, and she, seeming to know what I was thinking, said: 'Wouldn't it be lovely to adopt two young orphans from the Far East?' " Out of that conversation action came; and they said very simply that though the age difference was much greater, they felt they were getting even greater pleasure from the company of their new children than they had from their own family. I know of another home that has adopted six children, several of them black. In this particular family, there is nothing but harmony and joy.

Adoption is usually best done through a good agency, although private arrangements are possible. Whatever course is followed, both parents must take the little one completely to their hearts and love him with all the love they have to give. Environment is a far stronger force than heredity. If you can surround this little adopted child with faith and prayer, and with all that is godly and of good report, there is every reason to hope that there will emerge a fully committed Christian.

When will you tell him that he is adopted? And how? In general, the younger the better. And in telling him that you are not really his flesh-and-blood parents, you must simply stress that you *chose* him out of all the rest of the children in the world. Given a deep sense of your love, and being assured that your action in choosing him was the outflow of that love, he will discover in your company a close understanding of the everlasting love of the Father who "chose us in Christ before the foundation of the world." After all, "adoption" is one of the greatest Gospel words. Read Romans 8:15!

Is it wise to have a baby boy circumcised?

This is an important question.

When circumcision takes place, the prepuce or foreskin covering the head of the penis is removed. The head of the penis is thereby left exposed.

Circumcision has been practiced from ancient times. The procedure was regularly done in ancient Egypt and was common even among the Aztecs. Today, it is performed by many diverse groups—Australian aborigines, the Tacuna Indians of Brazil, Abyssinian Christians, and of course modern Jews and Moslems. The origin of the custom is unknown.

One reason for circumcision is cleanliness. In an uncircumcised penis, a cheeselike material called smegma can collect. This is secreted by the skin at the head of the penis. When the foreskin remains, this smegma collects and can become fruitful breeding ground for bacteria, with resultant infection. No known case of cancer of circumcised penis is listed in medical textbooks. If cancer does attack the penis, the only possible cure is amputation.

Many doctors advise circumcision and recommend that it be done before the baby leaves the hospital. You will have to take special care for a few days after reaching home if the wound has not completely healed. Covering the end of the penis with gauze coated with some kind of boric acid ointment or plain petroleum jelly should be adequate.

In adult life circumcision also adds to sexual pleasure. There is very little nerve supply in the foreskin; and with the head of the organ uncovered, much greater sensation is possible in contact with the vagina. On the whole, the arguments in favor of circumcision are very strong. If you feel it should be done, be sure to have it done in the earliest days of the child's life.

Are there some basic reactions on the part of the father that should be carefully watched?

There certainly are; though they are nothing like the basic reactions of grandparents, of which we shall speak in a moment.

Men react to pregnancy in their wives in most varied ways. Some immediately feel a deeper sense of protectiveness for their wife, along with an added sense of pride in their marriage. To men for whom virility is a matter of concern, there can come a heightened self-esteem. In most cases there is a strong sense of enjoyment in the anticipation of the birth of a child into the home.

Along with such signs, however, there can frequently be found a sense of being left out and neglected. This can express itself in a host of ways, from simple crossness to spending more time out of the home with male friends or even to flirtations with other women. Reactions of this kind are of course no help to the wife; and at this point we should stress what we have repeatedly stressed, namely, the need to act together as a couple, to bear and forbear with one another, to share the load whatever it may be, and in particular to determine that nothing is going to be allowed to enter and destroy what is pure and good.

This is an absolute basic for a Christian husband. There will be days, often in the first three months of pregnancy, when the wife feels far from well, and at a time like that there is no substitute for the consideration and care a husband can display. This is Christian duty. He should continually remember that whatever his feelings are, his wife's are all churned up as well. After the baby has come, the need for special consideration by the husband is vital. His wife has been through the equivalent of a surgical procedure; there has been considerable pain associated with it; and all this adds up to the wife's needing a great deal of aid and comfort from her husband at this time. If she is to give all that the baby ought to receive, then the mother must likewise receive more than usual. There are many areas in which this can be shown—in household chores, in cleaning up after meals, and in keeping a weather eye open for situations that might prove distracting to the mother. Even more than this, however, there is the moral support of appreciation, love, understanding, patience, courtesy and good humor. A crisis situation can so often be solved by making fun out of it. There are often times that a mother can become irritable and cross without any very obvious reason for it. Then, even more than ever, her husband can be to her a refuge and a strength and a very present help. If times arise when the wife is complaining, don't answer in the same manner. There may be reason for the complaint; there may not be. Whatever the situation, do try to be a help and not a hindrance.

Are grandparents a frequent cause of trouble at times like these?

Well, let's be grateful for what grandparents so often do for the best. For one thing, it is a great source of personal security for a child to know his grandparents. This is one of the things that helps give rootage in life. The sense of continuity and long life that grandparents can supply is really a major cause for gratitude.

Often, grandparents enjoy their grandchildren even more than they enjoyed their own children. There are obvious reasons for that. The ultimate responsibility for training and good behavior does not rest with them but on the parents; and usually, after a visit, the grandparents can leave the home where the children are and return to the peace of their own dwelling. While this is so, it is equally true that many a mother would have been harassed beyond all enduring had it not been for the presence of a wise grandparent. Be thankful for everything for which there is good reason to be grateful.

There are many parts of the world where grandmothers are counted as sages and experts. A young mother in lands of this kind naturally assumes that if a question rises in her mind about the baby or if she needs some special help for him, she will ask her mother. This is a very wonderful thing. Unfortunately, it doesn't obtain in every country. In our Western society we have become accustomed to referring to doctors and specialists and listening to them as though they were the very oracles of God. It is natural to assume that with the rapid advance of knowledge there are many things that even mother might not know. And in addition to this there is an urge on the part of young mothers, who may not be so very much younger than their own mothers, to demonstrate that they can do very well indeed without grand-parental control. Determined to be independent, they often reject much good and helpful advice.

What about jealousy in other members of the family?

We have really been talking about the first baby. But there is good reason to add a word on behalf of the other children in the family if this is not the first child.

The coming of a new baby affects the feelings of every member of the family at the deepest levels. Father and mother are of course deeply involved as we have already seen; but children share in the wonder of it all by thinking of themselves as parents too. There is astonishment, enthusiasm and something akin to awe in their reception of a new baby into the home. And yet, even in the most secure and loving of children there is also often a note of jealousy, of uneasiness, of suspicion and fear. These sparks of envy or hostility should be carefully watched. They don't rise from any genuine dislike, but from a basic fear of being left out, omitted, excluded. All that is needed is parental reassurance. If parents are wise, the petty rivalries for their affection will soon disappear in the children. If all is watched and safeguarded, there should be no problem at all. I have, however, seen a child of eighteen months lie on the floor and scream when a little cousin of hers came into the room. Somehow she had gotten the idea of being neglected, and this was her way of giving vent to her feelings. Even in this case, however, the two became, in the course of time, first tolerant of each other and then happy.

All this is part of the joy and interest of family life. In a Christian home there should never be any discrimination by any parent for or against any child. All should be loved equally well. They should know this. When they do, it is all the easier for the sense of the love of God to be accepted. And this, of course, is ultimately what the role of parents is: to stand in the place of God and to show forth His loving-kindness every day.

Is there anything else that a mother should know before having her first child?

Perhaps one thing more should be noted. New mothers experience a great letdown after the birth of the baby. This should be accepted as natural. Even though she looked forward eagerly to the birth of her child, the inexperienced mother may still suffer dismay when she again confronts the full responsibility of looking after her home—now with the added responsibility of a baby. She may become despondent a few days after getting home from the hospital. There, she was waited on hand and foot; but now, very abruptly, she is answerable to every whimper and cry that the baby may make, and responsible too for looking after her husband. In spite of all we have said about the father's showing particular care for his wife before and after pregnancy, it still remains true that a good percentage of men are babies at heart and depend far more on their wives than they will ever admit. At a time such as this, it is absolutely necessary that both husband and wife show great forbearance and that everything be done to ensure that all things work together for good. Where there is prayer, there will be care. A vicious circle of mother concentrating on the child while father feels left out must be avoided at all costs. A good piece of therapy is to make father care for the baby for a while. Try that, and see what happens!

One other thing a Christian parent should do. He should remember that it was as a little child the Saviour came. As Wesley says,

> God contracted to a span,
> Incomprehensibly made man.

To meditate at a time like this on the wonder of the everlasting love of God which gave His Son to be born of a pure virgin is rewarding and always uplifting. The depths and riches both of the wisdom and knowledge of God are past all telling; but they are always worthy of contemplation and they always reward the one who broods upon them. In *On the Trinity*, Novatian has a wonderful passage to help us envision a mode of being higher than anything we know in our familiar world of matter, space and time:

> Here and in all our meditations upon the qualities and content of God, we pass beyond the power of fit contemplation, nor can human eloquence put forth a power commensurate with His greatness. At the contemplation and utterance of His majesty all eloquence is rightly dumb, all mental effort is feeble. For God is greater than mind itself. His greatness cannot be conceived. Nay, could we conceive of His greatness He would be less than the human mind which could form the conception. He is greater than all language, and no statement can express Him. Indeed, if any statement could express Him, He would be less than human speech which could such statement comprehend and gather up all that He is. All our thoughts about Him will be less than He, and our loftiest utterances will be trivialities in comparison with Him.

Thoughts like these go through the mind of every Christian parent. I recall my first conversation with a proud father in one of my pastorates. He had just seen his first child for the first time, and all His thoughts were of the incredible wonder and glory of God. "To think that God has used Nancy and me to bring this to pass," he said, "makes me breathless with wonder." Then he added: "I don't think I have ever worshipped God so fully as I have just now."

Anything else?

Not really! I could of course say much more; but our main task at this point is completed. The first child in the home of committed Christians should be received as one of God's most marvellous gifts. You should treat as light banter the words of Christopher Fry in *A Sleep of Prisoners:*

> The moon is nothing
> But a circumambulatory aphrodisiac
> Divinely subsidised to provoke the world
> into a rising birth rate.

You should treat also as a very atypical piece of T. S. Eliot the following lines:

Birth, and copulation, and death.
That's all the facts when you come to brass tacks.

Not so! With every birth there begins a life that can move and arouse the world to behold God, a life that can emblazon in the skies of eternity a name that shall never pass away. When God shared with us this most priceless gift of creativity, He shared His own life. Too bad that so much of this most marvellous realization has gone from us! Quoting Eliot reminds me of some of his lines that are haunting in their sense of the tragic story of man. They come from *The Rock,* which he wrote in 1934.

All our knowledge brings us nearer to our ignorance,
All our ignorance brings us nearer to death,
But nearness to death no nearer to God.
Where is the life we have lost in living?
Where is the wisdom we have lost in knowledge?
Where is the knowledge we have lost in information?
The cycles of heaven in twenty centuries
Bring us farther from God and nearer to the Dust.

For a proper understanding of the meaning of birth, we must return to the creation ordinance God established at the dawning of time: "Be fruitful and replenish the earth." It is a divine privilege to become a parent. It is the greatest responsibility God could lay on any man or woman. Having given the gift of a child, He continues His mercy to them that love Him and keep His commandments. He covenants to lead and guide us *and our children* in His appointed way. He can do no more.

10: The Family

Is the idea of the family common to all mankind?

The answer is Yes. The family is a social grouping consisting of parents and children, and has been found in all societies either as the only form of corporate life or as the foundational unit in a larger and broader system. The primary functions of the family are protective, reproductive, economic and educational. In certain societies, such as those where polygamy is practiced, there exists what is known as the joint or extended family; and it is beyond question that a variety of excellent features are to be found in such societies. Care of the young and helpless, care of the old, care too of the immediate family of parents who may have suffered through illness or death—all these are characteristics from which our Western world could well learn. Among the Hebrews, Greeks and Romans, the patriarchal family was the norm. Indeed, in Rome only one person was recognized as an independent individual under the law. He was known as the *paterfamilias.* All religious rites were vested in him. All his family, including slaves, were under his total control; and inasmuch as his power extended to the taking of life, he really exercised the prerogatives of a monarch. When he died, all his property descended to his male heirs. There was very little alteration of this system either in canon or secular law until the nineteenth century, when Western nations began to grant rights to women as well as to men. Under the impact of the industrial revolution, there was a heightened breakdown of the family system. Work that had previously been done within the family circle, such as cooking, baking, weaving and spinning, was done by others, increasingly destroying the true unity of family life. The secular city, too, has taken its toll on the family. Anyone interested in the growth and development of family life should consult such major works as E. R. and G. H. Groves, *The Contemporary American Family* (1947); S. A. Queen, *The Family in Various Cultures*(1952); W. F. Kenkel, *The Family in Perspective*(1960); and the three volumes of A. W. Calhoun, *A Social History of the American Family* (1960). The breakdown of family life that has marked our twentieth century is adduced by sociologists and psychologists as one of the principal germs of maladjustment which is having so great a bearing on subjects so diverse as mental hygiene, education and divorce.

There is a specific Christian teaching re the family, isn't there?

Of course there is. The holy family in Nazareth is among the greatest examples. There we read that "Jesus was subject unto His parents" and that "He increased in wisdom and stature and in favour with God and men" (Luke 2:52). The ideal family life illustrated in the Old Testament is carried forward into the New Testament and is given fresh approval. The fourth commandment to "Honour your father and mother" is made specific in the New Testament. There is no annulling of that law. Indeed, when Paul writes to the church in Ephesus, immediately after the great passage we have already quoted regarding husbands and wives and the way in which marriage is a mirror of the union of Christ with His Church, he makes the following admonition to children:

> Children, the right thing for you to do is to obey your parents as those whom the Lord has set over you. Remember, the first commandment to contain a promise was
>
> Honour thy father and thy mother
> That it may be well with thee
> and that thou mayest live long on the earth.

And no sooner has Paul made this statement, than he adds a word to fathers:

> Fathers, don't over-correct your children or make it difficult for them to obey the commandment. Bring them up with Christian teaching in Christian discipline.

The word for family or families occurs nearly 300 times in the Bible.

What is the really dominant fact in family life?

Copying. At least it ought to be. Children need friendly and helpful parents. And deep in the breast of every child is a longing to have a mother or father who is worth copying. Unfortunately, too many of us fail here. We can offer a thousand excuses, but none of them will make up for the loss of a real copy. Let me amplify.

A daughter needs a friendly father if she is to develop naturally. There is no need for her to pattern herself after him; but she should be sure that her actions are approved. This is one of the great ways in which she acquires self-confidence and a true sense of identity. Approval can be shown in the simplest ways: by saying how well she is driving the car, by admiring her hairdo, by thanking her for helping Mother. He can share his thoughts with her and ask for her reactions. By thus learning the qualities that belong in family life and particularly those parts that are truly masculine, she is really being prepared for the day when she will take a husband to herself. The kind of man with whom she will ultimately fall in love is determined to a far greater degree than is generally realized by the relationship, good or bad, right or wrong, that she has had with her father.

Similarly, a boy needs someone to copy. But right here we run into the age-old problem of sons' being separated from their fathers because of a lack of communication. Perhaps the father is intolerant and domineering, making real companionship impossible. If such a breakdown has occurred, a boy may learn to lead a double life, becoming extremely adept at such a Jekyll and Hyde existence. Should this ever happen, it is unfortunate in the extreme; and every father should search his heart constantly to see if there is anything that he is consciously or unconsciously doing to alienate his son. It may happen that the father is determined to see his son succeed in school, or in sports, or in some special area of the arts. If the effect is to make the boy feel uncomfortable, or to make him feel that he can never quite make it, he is going to be under pressure continually, and the results can be disastrous. Many a potentially happy home has been destroyed by the overzealousness of a father eager to see his son do well. Better a thousand times to come short of perfection and to have a happy, confidential association with one another than to reap the harvest of separation and family breakup.

In the earliest periods of their lives, little children (especially between the years of three and six) are inspired by and pattern themselves after their parents. It may well be that they overglamorize their parents' gifts and capacities. But, in the main, a boy wants to be like his father, and he will imitate his father's actions in dozens of ways. Similarly with girls! They want to be like their mothers—in style, in action, and in having babies. Both boys and girls develop a romantic attachment for the parent of the opposite sex. The boy's affection for his mother may, in fact, lead him to a growing antagonism toward his father. This is the theme of Sophocles' *Oedipus Rex.* After this stage, sexuality goes underground in a sense, and romantic attraction turns to aversion. The boy passes through a stage in which he has no time for girls, squirms away from kisses by his mother, and turns to other interests—hobbies, reading, nature or science. Likewise, girls giggle in the presence of boys and usually shun their company. But through these years, boy and girl alike are developing emotionally and moving toward the stage of adolescence, when major glandular changes take place that are convulsive and often traumatic.

It is at this stage that any latent rebelliousness against parental control reveals itself and is compounded by the earlier sense of dependence on the parents. Defiant moods can become intense and exaggerated, and, as we see so frequently today, children from the best of homes may escape to hippie communes, where they find nothing of the old parental restraints and feel correspondingly free to associate in complete liberty with total strangers.

As Jung says in his *Psychological Aspects of the Modern Archetype* (1938), "Emotion is the chief source of all becoming-conscious. There can be no transforming of darkness into light and of apathy into movement without emotion." It must be a constant prayer of Christian parents that by some divine alchemy even their mistakes will be made to work together for the good of their children. It is still the dominant fact that the child will follow where the parents lead—if *their* dependence has been entirely upon God. It should never be forgotten that God has pledged His word in this: "Train up a child in the way that he should go, and when he is old, he will not depart therefrom" (Proverbs 22:6). Claim that promise for your children. Pray that you may be a true example to them of godliness, trustworthiness, goodness and humor. If that be so, there should be little fear about the outcome.

Do you believe in a lot of permissiveness in family life?

How much is "a lot"? This certainly is a big question for many new parents. And the problems don't decrease as more children are added to the family and as they grow older. Family attitudes on this subject have changed enormously throughout history. Variations in the severity of upbringing have been as numerous as the ages themselves. Time was when children were actually seen and not heard. But great changes have taken place. Educationists, psychologists and medical doctors have all done independent researches, and the results have been surprisingly uniform. It is a generally accepted educational premise that a child learns better and faster with a method that is positive rather than negative, that encourages rather than restrains, that is open rather than evasive. It is now common knowledge that harsh toilet training or frightening stories told in answer to a child's natural questions about sex can lead to real distortions of personality and possibly neurosis. And it is quite the custom now for doctors to encourage mothers to allow babies to determine their own feeding times. All this is comparatively new.

But the basic question hasn't yet been faced. Granted that our knowledge has advanced and that we have a better methodology in many areas of child education, is it easy for a parent to change over from the way in which he himself was reared? It may be comparatively easy to pick up new ideas about certain things and to recognize their worth; but to pass through a fundamental change that would transform a parent who had been reared strictly with regard to honesty, obedience, manners, sex and truthfulness is possibly too much to expect from the normal parent. The result is that many parents are confused about this question of what to permit and what to forbid. Some parents may feel that they were themselves too strictly brought up; and their natural attitude may be to go along with a much more permissive course. This is the kind of thing that can then happen. You allow the child to behave as he wants and you get angry about it. But because of your past, and your determination not to do to your child what was done to you, you let it pass; yet all the time you feel guilty a bit, and possibly the sense of guilt increases as the years roll by when you find your children unresponsive to any correction at all.

Perhaps Dr. Spock is right when he says that "strictness and permissiveness are not the real issues; that good-hearted parents who aren't afraid to be firm when necessary can get good results with either moderate strictness or moderate permissiveness; and that on the other hand, a strictness that comes from harsh feelings or a permissiveness that is timid and vacillating can each lead to poor results" (*Common Sense Book*, 1957). Certainly for any Christian parent there is a very real problem. As society becomes more un-Christian, and as our children grow up in an environment that boasts of its casting off the old ways because the new freedoms are infinitely better, it is not easy to know how to advise them aright. Certainly, obedience must be taught and respect for honesty and truth. Every boy and girl should be trained to hate a lie and to pursue purity of life. If this is to be, there must be much prayer at the family altar. There must be prayer that will pursue our children as they go out to college and into the world of business and the professions. And this prayer takes time. The Christian parent lays hold on God and says repeatedly, "I will not let Thee go except Thou bless me—and my children." One of the most heartening signs in many parts of our continent at this time is the growth of prayer cells in the homes of church members. It is good to know that at many of these groups, parents are praying earnestly for the protection and deliverance of their children from the snare and power of the devil. This is the way to victory. This is the kind of action that makes great saints possible even in our times.

Permissiveness is unknown when we are determined to seek only the "good, and perfect, and acceptable will of God" (Romans 12:1). If there is this kind of desire, then the whole life becomes one torrent of desire to know the living God and to pursue Him till He be found. I would encourage a mighty longing after God. For lack of it, our churches languish. Complacency is the deadly foe of spiritual growth. But God waits to be wanted. He is willing to "do far more and exceeding abundantly beyond what we ask or think" (Ephesians 3:20). Unfortunately we live in an era of religious complexity. Christ does not dominate our lives or our thoughts. In our churches we have programs and more programs, but far too little pursuit of God.

How much discipline should there be exercised by parents in their families?

A hard question. There is certainly a lot of misunderstanding about the advantages and disadvantages of discipline. A great deal of study has been spent on this subject by educators, psychiatrists and pediatricians. Their results have often been contradictory; and this, possibly more than anything else, has confused parents. After all, they say, if the experts can't agree, how can we succeed?

Some things, however, are definite. Let me list them. For one thing, all children need the love and security of their parents' presence if they are to develop naturally. Many children who do get into trouble are really suffering from lack of affection rather than from lack of discipline. And unconscious thoughts are as influential as conscious ones. Further, most children want to learn and are able to do so if the teaching given is accommodated to their age and inclinations. In this connection I should emphasize that sex is an entirely natural interest of children, and that when they ask questions about it, they should be given clear and forthright answers, though of course answers that take some account of their age. Another point worth stressing is that there are no children who do not at some time or other have jealous or angry feelings toward their brothers and sisters and parents. Finally, since every child is an individual in his own right, he should be given every opportunity to develop in his own way.

If these things are understood, and if the child is blessed with parents who have acclimatized themselves to these generally accepted ideas, then discipline should be carefully delimited within fixed boundaries. It is possible to be both firm and loving at the same time. It is possible to say to a child that there will be a penalty for breaking one of the family laws and yet at the same time let him understand that this is for his good.

Even in the circle of his own home, a spoiled child is not a happy one. To counter any possibility of spoiling the child, it is wise to have a set of home rules that are easily understandable with penalties for breaking the rules that are acknowledged as fair. In any home where the parents are prepared to let their children get away with anything, and perhaps even encouraging them to do so, there is little hope that a true family will be built. Families are founded on mutual understanding, trust and courtesy. Loyalty to one's word should be demanded of every child always; for truthfulness is the greatest gift we can implant in our children. If this is to be, however, the parent must never promise what he cannot fulfill or fail to fulfill what he has promised. The God of the Bible is a God who cannot lie. And every parent who stands before the children of his home *in loco dei* must be equally true to his word and bond.

In discipline within the family, there should—indeed there must—be complete agreement between both parents. There is nothing worse than for a child to know that the mother will wink at what the father condemns, or vice versa. It is crucial to the basic chemistry of children that they know when they have displeased their parents and when they deserve some fitting penalty. Be the penalty what it may, both parents must be at one concerning it. Otherwise, the family health is being sadly impaired. What's more, see to it that when the penalty has been met, the incident is completely forgotten. And never forget that it is the total atmosphere of the family that really matters. To love and be loved in return should be the goal of all family life—even if discipline is involved.

How much sex education should be given at home?

As much as possible. It is far better for it to be given there than in school. The family is the natural arena for learning the facts of life, and parents are unsurpassed as teachers in this area if they really work hard at it. This is implied in the Book of Proverbs where Solomon says:

> My son, do not forget my teaching,
> but guard my commands in your heart;
> for long life and years in plenty
> will they bring you, and prosperity as well.

> Let your good faith and loyalty never fail,
> but bind them about your neck.
> Thus will you win favour and success
> in the sight of God and man.
> Put all your trust in the Lord
> and do not rely on your own understanding.
> Think of Him in all your ways,
> and He will smooth your path.
> Do not think how wise you are,
> but fear the Lord and turn from evil.
> Let that be the medicine to you in health,
> the liniment for your limbs (New English Bible).

The general counsel is clear. A wise couple will attend to the training of their children in things both mental and physical—including sexual.

Children are naturally reticent to discuss aspects of their sex life with their parents; and it is never easy to know whether to wait until you are asked some question or to take the initiative and offer the instruction you feel will be helpful. Both methods should be followed, I think, and there ought to be regular reliance on the guidance of the Holy Spirit as to when and where and how to introduce topics that are essentially very private. Parents must respect the innate modesty of their children. At the same time, the children may be longing for you to tell them plainly some of the things they are hesitant to ask. Pray that you will be led in the right way to speak the right word to the right person at the right time. He is a wise man who can do that. Begin early; little children are vitally interested in every part of their bodies. Gain confidence, for yourself and from them, and there should in the end be no real problem.

That's all right; but you haven't fully answered the question, which was: How much sex education should be given at home? Can you be more explicit?

Of course. I said that *as much as possible* sex education should be given at home, but perhaps that should be developed a little in some specific matters.

Parents should teach their children to aim for uninhibited sex;

and that means letting them know that some things can't be hurried. Something can easily be destroyed if you start with sex too soon; and it is a very wise thing to sacrifice what you may want right now in order to be sure of getting what you will want in the future. Kicks have kickbacks. Be sure your children know the worthwhileness of waiting for God's best.

A mother should prepare her daughter mentally and emotionally for the changes that will take place in her body when she comes to an age of about eleven to thirteen. There may be a biology class at school at which some of this is taught. So far so good! But be sure that the right emphasis is being made and at the right time. Every girl should be mentally prepared for menstruation; but please do this in the most natural way possible and be positive all the time. Emphasizing the troublesome aspects of the phenomenon never helps. Tell her that it is as universal as woman is; every girl has the right to know why it happens, how it happens, and what she should do when it happens. If the girl is told that through menstruation she is being prepared for motherhood, she will welcome it rather than be repelled by it. Be wholesome and happy in describing it. She will be grateful all life long for what you did.

Masturbation and its effects, both beneficial and harmful, should be openly dealt with. The word comes from a root—*masturbari*—that means "polluting oneself." But there is no medical ground whatsoever for believing that masturbation, which is simple stimulation of the genital areas, to produce an orgasm outside of sexual relations, is harmful in any way. Masturbation is a substitute form of gratification when sexual intercourse is impossible. This form of self-stimulation is possible for girls as well as for boys, though it is much less common. Further, girls are more prone to stimulate themselves by rubbing their legs against playground equipment such as swings and slides. They also find that climbing trees and sliding down ropes or poles are also effective means of stimulating their genitals. For boys the process is simple. All that is required is gentle manipulation of the end of the penis.

Is there anything harmful in this? Medically, as I have just said, there is not. No scientific research has ever demonstrated that bodily damage results from it. In adolescence there is a pronounced increase in the practice of masturbation for obvious reasons. The increasing function of the glands affects not only the body but the mind and the imagination. The result is that the youth becomes increasingly conscious of a driving force within him compelling him to think along sexual and romantic lines. It is a very easy step from there to finding release through self-stimulation.

We must face the question openly. Is this likely to do the young person any abiding injury? Certainly, guilt and worry are very often associated with it. The problem is compounded by a host of sexual imageries that may fill the mind while this is being practiced; and these can certainly be troublesome and harmful. My own feeling is that with care, and at periods when obviously there is a tremendous overflow of surging sexual powers within him, it is better for a boy to relieve himself than to go out and try to seduce or rape a girl. The quick surge of hormones that occurs during puberty causes most dramatic changes in the sexual organs as well as the sexual feelings. The whole period is one of preoccupation with sex. Clearly, God intended it so. It is universal. But what we must warn our young people against is the thinking of sexual scenes at such times. The condition of their mind is all-important. They may imagine all types of situations in which they are mixed up with the other sex. This certainly is where the real trouble can lie. It is possible to think oneself into situations through which one would never actually go. And it is here that a deep sense of guilt may permeate any procedure in masturbation. It is impossible to say that such thoughts of guilt spring from the type of home or culture in which the child has been reared. They are far too universal for this to be the case. Any association during masturbation with thoughts of what is fundamentally improper, unchaste and immoral will obviously create the type of tension to which we are referring.

My own counsel through the years has been that young people should not practice this if they can get along without practicing it. But if the impulse becomes overpowering, then they should relieve themselves as clinically and as cleanly as possible. This is something that a youth understands and I have always found a response of gratitude when this kind of guidance has been given. A youth certainly should be told why it is that at this stage of his life this sudden urge comes over him. He should know it is a universal condition, that it signifies he is growing up naturally, and that if it were not so there would be cause for concern. There is one verse from St. Paul that I press on young people when talking of this experience. It is II Corinthians 10:5: "Casting down imaginations, and everything that exalteth itself against the knowledge of God, and bringing into captivity every thought to the obedience of Christ." That is a wonderful verse of Scripture. It contains the promise that every evil thought, every fashion of perverse imagination, can be brought under the dominion of Jesus Christ. This is the birthright of the Christian, and he should possess his possessions.

Some young people, through vigorous sports, by taking cold showers, or by going for long walks or jogs when they feel this surge developing, are able to cope with it without too great difficulty. It certainly is an area in which our young people can, and very heroically too, practice a form of self-denial that will significantly develop their characters. Not many succeed completely in overcoming the practice. But don't be dismayed. You are not alone. Every youth with health bursting in his body is having to cope with what you are meeting too. Treat it in the healthiest possible way; pray for guidance at times when you feel you need special grace to help you win through to some significant victory; and carve your own pathway upwards towards God. He will never fail you. He will always prove to be a "refuge in the time of storm, as a shadow of a great rock in a weary land."

One thing that is very foolish is for a parent to say to his son: "Do this; but don't do it too often." Such qualified consent without associated reasons and other ideals can be very disconcerting. Parents should tell their sons that nocturnal emissions, which are very common at this period of life, along with natural erection of the penis, are normal and universal. What the average youth wants at this stage of his life is reassurance that he is not a freak or a subnormal member of the human species. But whatever else you do, be it mother or father speaking to daughter or son, please don't stress the harmful and dangerous aspects of sex. This is a common failing of parents who have themselves been strictly reared in fear of sex. A nervous mother may make her daughter fearful of becoming pregnant. A father may warn about the dangers of contracting venereal disease. On the whole this stress can cause more harm than good. Wholesomeness of conversation and a deep and broad assurance that what is happening is natural and is being naturally opened up in the family for each member of the family to know and understand the wonderful ways in which God has made us for Himself—all this will repay dividends of untold value in years to come. There is no reason in the world why this subject should not be treated in the most natural and beautiful way.

Anything more to be added?

Perhaps this. There is a very wonderful word in the Bible which reads, "God setteth the solitary in families" (Psalm 68:6). I take that to mean that God plants us as individual persons in families in order that in the circle of the family we should develop and grow to the very highest of our potential. The Psalmist continues in the same verse with these words: "He brings out those who are bound with chains." This phrase has been variously interpreted. The New English Bible makes it refer quite simply to bringing out prisoners safe and sound. But there can well be a much deeper meaning here. It is in families that God expands our personalities. It is God's intent that through family life we should be nurtured to full maturity of body and spirit. And in this wonderful process of growth within a family circle, we can be set free from many types of bondage which the fatherless and the homeless know.

Our Lord was reared within a family. We are told very little of what went on in the family at Nazareth, but Jesus was subject unto his parents and learned from them continually. By His birth into a family, He consecrated all true family life. In following Him, we should be glad and rejoice that this has been our privilege; and we should do everything in our power to make our family life a thing of joy. This should be the goal of all parents. This should be the end towards which all sex and marriage tends—the creation of a family where Christ is indeed the head of the house, the unseen guest at every meal, the silent listener to every conversation.

Happy the home when God is there,
    And love fills every breast,

Where one their wish, and one their prayer,
And one their heavenly rest.

God make all our homes like this. In them His praise will continually be heard.

Have you any advice about family finances?

Lots! And that there is much need for advice here is shown by divorce statistics, which list money as one of the chief culprits in home breakups.

Money in itself is not an evil thing. The right of private possession is recognized clearly in the Bible. But when money becomes an end in itself, it can be a very devilish thing. By placing a penny near enough to your eye you can close out the sun. So money, if wrongly sought and used, can displace God from the central throne of our spirits. "Seek first the kingdom of God and His righteousness, and all other things will be added unto you" (Matthew 6:33).

Whatever else happens in your home, be sure that as husband and wife you work out your financial affairs together. There may not be a great deal to go around. There may be times when you have trouble making ends meet. But if you agree to have no secrets from one another in matters of finance, the way will be very much sweeter. In the wonderful passage in Proverbs 31, the mother of the home is shown as the financial director; and this can sometimes be a very wonderful thing. You may be blessed with a wife who is better than you are at handling money. If so, let her do it. Better, however, if you do things together. Make the mortgage payments together. Let your funds and finances be a source of real fun. Budget for your needs and budget wisely; but above all else, budget together. I know a home where the husband gives his wife twenty dollars a week to keep the house and clothe the children. He keeps all the rest and his wife has no idea of what he does with it. This is utter folly and totally forbidden for the Christian.

Then too, give God His part of all your income. You must think that through together also. Some give a tithe. Some give much more. Give as you are able and don't forget that "the Lord loves a cheerful giver" (II Corinthians 9:7). Teach your children the joy of giving to God. You can teach them nothing more wonderful.

11: Sexual Perversions

I am glad you are planning to say something about sexual perversion, for there seems to be a great deal of it; but I know only a very little. First of all, has the Bible anything to say about this?

It certainly has. Paul's letter to the Romans was called by Coleridge "the profoundest book in existence," and Martin Luther in his famous preface says: "This Epistle is the chief book of the New Testament and the purest gospel." Well, in the very first chapter of this amazing book, Paul speaks a great deal about sexual perversity, condemns it outright, and shows the kind of things that happen when men and women indulge in them.

I never knew that. Can you read the passage?

Well, let's take it part by part. His great argument begins at verse 18 of the first chapter after establishing that although God had revealed Himself plainly to men in the universe around them, mankind refused to recognize his existence and thank Him for all His gifts. The result of this was that

> They became fatuous in their argumentations, and plunged their silly minds still further into the dark. Behind a facade of "wisdom" they became just fools, fools who would exchange the glory of the eternal God for an imitation image of a mortal man, or of creatures that run or fly or crawl. They gave up God: and therefore God gave them up—to be the playthings of their own foul desires in dishonoring their own bodies (Phillips).

This is Paul's preamble to his great statement on moral and sexual perversity. And note! It all stems from a refusal to acknowledge God as God and to worship Him in spirit and in truth.

He proceeds:

> These men deliberately forfeited the Truth of God and accepted a lie, paying homage and giving service to the creature instead of to the Creator, who alone is worthy to be worshiped for ever and ever, Amen. God therefore handed them over to disgraceful passions.

The sequence is most significant. "They gave up God." "God gave them up." Note the development:

> Their women exchanged the normal practices of sexual intercourse for something which is abnormal and unnatural. Similarly the men, turning from natural intercourse with women, were swept into lustful passions for one another. Men with men performed these shameful horrors, receiving, of course, in their own personalities the consequences of sexual perversity.

Out of this there develop a host of other evils which you can read about for yourself. Enough, however, has been read to show that in writing these words in the first century Paul was in actual fact addressing every century, and not least our own. For all that he describes as happening in his time throughout the Roman Empire, and as going back through history to the first days of man's rebellion against God, is as up to date as today's newspaper. It is extraordinary that there is no sin that we know of today that is not catalogued at some point in the Bible. The consequences of deliberate atheism are always fearful.

Well, what exactly is meant by these words of Paul?

He is describing the world of homosexuality. The union of man with woman is known as a heterosexual act. Homosexuality refers to sexual relations between people of the same sex.

What is lesbianism?

It is female homosexuality. As Paul says, "Their women exchanged the normal practices of sexual intercourse for something which is abnormal and unnatural." This occurs sometimes under an irresistible attraction of one woman for another. They wish to be continually together and they practice mutual masturbation with one another. Most prostitutes are female homosexuals in their private lives. But lesbianism is by no means confined to them. You will find it at times in the most unexpected quarters—in areas indeed where it is the very last thing you would expect. After many years in the ministry, I thought recently that I could no longer be shocked. But not so. In conversation with a lady whom I had never suspected, I was more than amazed to discover that lesbianism was a controlling passion with her and that, try as she might, she had been unable to break with the habit.

It is of course impossible for two females to have full intercourse with one another. But by a rhythmic manipulation of the genital areas of one another it is possible to achieve orgasm. This can be done simultaneously, or subsequently to one another. What's more, the mouth is used both for kissing the lips and breasts and for licking the genital areas (cunnilingus). Thus, fondling and caressing one another, hugging and squeezing their bodies together, an illusion of romance in sexual involvement is created. There are many lesbians who believe that they can do in one hour for another woman what no man could accomplish in ten years. That is the kind of claim they make. But it is unnatural. It is not what God intended for male and female. When God made man, He made them male and female and He made them for one another. It is a tragic delusion when women seek in their own kind the satisfaction God planned that they obtain from someone of the opposite sex.

Tell us something about male homosexuality.

Well, this is really a dreary wilderness. The number of homosexuals has of course been rising greatly in the past generation, and there are many reasons for that. They are known as the "gay" people. Male homosexuality is a state in which men have a compelling emotional and sexual interest in other men. There are of course obstacles and in many cases homosexuals will resort to all kinds of ingenuity in order to satisfy one another. Frequently they attire themselves as women, wear make-up, adopt female mannerisms and the like. For long years the practice of homosexuality has been treated by many nations as a criminal act. In cases where an adult practiced his operations on younger boys, the offense was considered very serious indeed, and extensive periods of imprisonment were the usual punishment. Indeed one of the saddest experiences I have ever known was taking part in a church service in a maximum security prison and having one of the prisoners as soloist. He had recently been found guilty of sodomy (as homosexuality is frequently called), and he sang "I have a mighty Saviour." The really tragic part about the situation was that he was a well-known Christian evangelist but had fallen into this temptation and been caught in the act. His "mighty Saviour" had been forgotten when he gave himself over to acts like these.

Recently, however, there has been a tremendous easing of opinion about this, and the Christian Church is even being asked to perform the ceremony of Christian marriage between homosexuals. There is a church in Los Angeles for homosexuals only. Not so long ago, I saw a cartoon illustrating "wives' visiting day" at prison; but all who were trooping out of the bus into the prison were men. Legislation is being eased in many countries, and penalties are scarcely known now for the practice. Homosexual acts between consenting adults have in fact been legalized in various parts of the world.

What do homosexuals do to one another?

It is just as well that you should know. Apart from a very great quantity of frilly things with the use of female garments and the like, they basically promote mutual masturbation. They undress, get into bed, manipulate each other's penis to the point of orgasm, and the main show is over. A very few minutes is all that is required.

One particularly odious practice is known as fellatio. This is intercourse by the mouth. One man will suck the penis of the other. Indeed, in some cases this is the only way in which orgasm can be reached. When one is satisfied, the roles are reversed. Homosexual contacts are usually very impersonal. A man will go out questing for another of his kind. This is known as "cruising." They recognize one another by an uncanny empathy and can quickly make whatever rendezvous they want—frequently a men's washroom. Afterwards, they may never see one another again. This is in contrast to those more enduring types of which I have already spoken.

Is that all there is to homosexuality?

Apart from the frills, as I have already said, this is what happens. Any homosexual may have as many as four or five different experiences in one night—and the partners are usually different. Robbery, assault and blackmail are commonplace among the homosexual community. Sometimes, through disagreements as to sexual proceedings, there can be savage beatings; and every police vice squad in the country knows what to expect in certain areas of their beat. Sadism and masochism also are found, but the practicing homosexual will do his best to avoid anyone who likes this kind of thing. They have an instinct that often saves them from grievous bodily harm. There is no doubt that men who combine homosexuality with sadism are the most cruel of people. They were the men who found professional employment in ancient times as torturers and executioners. In recent times they moved in the ranks of Hitler's Gestapo and SS. Terror and intimidation are their stock in trade.

Is there anything more that homosexuals do?

Because they are men and possess the same organs, homosexuals must use their imagination to the full; and they certainly do. They will lie one on top of the other with the penis firmly enclosed in the tightly held legs of the lower partner. Or they will rub against one another, thigh to thigh, abdomen to abdomen, until some climax is reached. Some go one step further and insert the penis into the anus of the partner. Generous amounts of lubricating jelly are often used, but even this does not prevent considerable pain for the "female" partner. Anything is used to create a climax.

Since homosexuals are capable of prodigious promiscuity, sooner or later a homosexual is going to make contact with someone with venereal disease. This has added to the complication of trying to root out VD, for homosexual contacts are so casual it is almost impossible to trace anything back to its source.

being a new creature with the mind of Christ illumining his redeemed personality. Yes! There is cure for every type of sin and cleansing at the Cross. We must despair of none.

Would this be the place to ask about prostitution?

I think so. Prostitution is known as the oldest profession. It certainly has been around for a long time.

Prostitution exists as a commercialized system whereby women hire out their bodies for the sexual gratification of men. It has a most varied history. Among the ancient Chinese, Greeks, Cypriots and Armenians, prostitution was held in high esteem. It played a most important part in many of the ancient religions. Almost every temple had its own horde of official prostitutes, and intercourse with them was regarded as part of the religious ceremony—for a fee of course! Armenians and Cypriots made a practice of encouraging their daughters to indulge in prostitution in order to earn their dowry money. Prostitution continues today. Some countries have outlawed it, notably the Communist countries of eastern Europe. But the profession is practiced in almost every other country, with greater or lesser toleration by the police. In Mexico, prostitution has been legalized for a long time.

It is commonly held that professional prostitution is one of the principal carriers of venereal disease. It is difficult to substantiate this claim. In Mexico, for example, the incidence of venereal disease is much lower than in the United States, a country which tries to suppress it. Risk of VD from prostitutes is low. A 1966 survey in New York of 4700 women arrested for prostitution revealed remarkably that only 0.8 per cent of them had syphilis. When it is remembered that only the lowest rung of street prostitutes fall into the hands of the police, and that the call girl in her highly decorated apartment is scarcely ever brought into this kind of survey, the argument for a high spread of VD through this profession hardly stands up.

Prostitution is degrading, however, is it not?

Undoubtedly. Granted that most of the customers of prostitutes are married men who have not been sexually fulfilled by their wives, it is still true that the willingness of women to sell their bodies for money is a disgusting and demoralizing thing. It has no place in the Christian ethic. That should be stated bluntly and categorically. Indeed, one of the most dramatic poems in the entire Old Testament is a warning against enticement into the parlors of the prostitute. It merits quotation in full at this point, as I have found many who are ignorant of it. You find it in Proverbs 7:6-27:

> I glanced out of the window of my house,
> I looked through the lattice,
> and I saw among the simple youths,
> there among the boys I noticed
> a lad, a foolish lad,
> passing along the street, at the corner,
> stepping out in the direction of her house
> at twilight, as the day faded,
> at dusk as the night grew dark;
> suddenly a woman came to meet him,
> dressed like a prostitute, full of wiles,
> flighty and inconstant,
> a woman never content to stay at home,
> lying in wait at every corner,
> now in the street, now in the public squares.
> She caught hold of his hand and kissed him;
> brazenly she accosted him and said,
> "I have had a sacrifice, an offering, to make
> and I have paid my vows today;
> that is why I have come out to meet you,
> to watch for you and find you.
> I have spread coverings in my bed
> of coloured linen from Egypt.
> I have sprinkled my bed with myrrh,
> my clothes with aloes and cassia.
> Come, let us drown ourselves in pleasure,
> let us spend a whole night in love;
> for the man of the house is away,
> he has gone on a long journey,
> he has taken a bag of silver with him;
> until the moon is full he will not be home."

Persuasively she led him on,
she pressed him with seductive words.
Like a simple fool he followed her,
like an ox on its way to the slaughterhouse,
like an antelope bounding into the noose,
like a bird hurrying into the trap;
he did not know that he was risking his life
until the arrow pierced his vitals.

But now, my son, listen to me,
attend to what I say.
Do not let your heart entice you
into her ways,
do not stray down her paths;
many has she pierced and laid low,
and her victims are without number.
Her house is the entrance to Sheol,
which leads down to the halls of death.

When Paul writes of the glory of the Holy Spirit's indwelling the mortal body of every believer, he says:

> Have you realized the almost incredible fact that your bodies are integral parts of Christ Himself? Am I then to take parts of Christ and join them to a prostitute? Never! Don't you realize that when a man joins himself to a prostitute he makes with her a physical unity?

Babylon is known in the Book of Revelation as the "Mother of Prostitution," and John heard the Church Triumphant rejoicing as she fell from her place of dominion and power down to the darkness of hell itself. There is no place at all in the Christian ethic for contact with prostitutes. That goes also for any hint of extra-marital sexual intercourse or any kind of pre-marital intercourse. They are all of the same breed. They are all alike condemned by the Word of God and by the Lord of that Word.

How does a girl begin to act as a prostitute?

Usually because she likes it and finds it an easy way to make money. It can begin with a period of regular promiscuity because she simply likes that way of life. There may follow a marriage with divorce. Then, a job as waitress in a night club or as bar maid. Casual sex with suitable payment naturally follows, and there are always professional hustlers around who are only too ready to encourage such arrangements. When this happens, the girl is firmly embarked on the life.

But we spoke of degradation? What form does it take?

For a time, girls may make good money at this game, though their expenses are always high. Eventually, however, they find the allure of alcohol to be very great. And is there any more pitiable sight than an alcoholic hooker? Now, in our contemporary society, the awful pull of drugs has taken over. Drugs may be easy to come by or they may be hard, but invariably they cost money. The prostitute who is hooked on drugs will do almost anything to secure the needed fix. Often she lives with a procurer or pimp, as he is commonly referred to. The pimp lives from the earnings of his girl friend, always seeing to it that he gets his cut out of the girl's earnings—and a big one too. If the girl falls on bad times, he may simply take over another, more successful girl. His one-time girl friend is simply thrown out the door.

It should be said that top-grade prostitutes avoid drugs, for they realize only too well how dangerous they are. They have seen that the first step down in the case of many other girls was the start with drugs. On the other hand, many females who are on drugs turn to prostitution to pay for their habit. Occasionally real professionals may take some amphetamines or pep pills to keep going during a major convention, but they do try to avoid everything else. But whether they avoid drugs or not, in the end the tale is bitter. There is no personal satisfaction for the girl who lives in this way, for she knows that the mere passage of time will ultimately disqualify her. Few of them are able to save enough money against old age, and the end of the road is dreary and sad.

Are there other forms of sexual perversion?

There are; but it is doubtful if there is any point in going into them in detail. There are areas of suburbia where sexual mores permit a quite open promiscuity. Sexual intercourse is practiced with different partners and at various times apart from the marriage bond. Indeed, it was only yesterday that I read in one of our better-class journals about parties where men and women undressed—supposedly it was all a game—and then proceeded to mingle sexually with one another. Many of the hippie communes that have grown up around us are distinguished by this free-love kind of life. But such a mode of living is actually worse than that of animals. Indeed, it cannot be denied that there are animals and birds who are more exclusive and restrained in their behavior to their own kind. One of the great judgments of God on this generation is that there are few great writers who can rise above the appeals of passion and sex to present truly great literature to our times. On the contrary, men and women with gifts of writing have prostituted their pens or their typewriters to the exaltation of pure pornography. It is one of the saddest commentaries on our generation that we lack in the Western world people of herculean stature in literature who can withstand the urge to appeal to the sated and degraded instincts of the reading public. If there be true genius in our times, it hasn't followed the highest star. Ah, for a new gift of writing such as Shakespeare's!

Let me not to the marriage of true minds
Admit impediments. Love is not love
Which alters when it alteration finds,
Or bends with the remover to remove;
Oh no! it is an ever fixed mark,
That looks on tempests and is never shaken;
It is the star to every wandering bark,
Whose worth's unknown, although his height be taken.
Love's not Time's fool, though rosy lips and cheeks
Within his bending sickle's compass come;
Love alters not with his brief hours and weeks,
But bears it out even to the edge of doom:—
If this be error and upon me proved,
I never writ, nor no man ever loved.

Is there anything else that should be said about these things?

Yes, most certainly. The Christian couple confronted with

anything like this must turn from it like the plague. What is more, they may possibly come into contact with people who are committed homosexuals—they turn up in all kinds of quarters—and it is necessary to be forewarned. First of all, you must know that the real secret of living a life of purity is to allow the Holy Spirit to indwell all your heart and mind. The Holy Spirit will reveal Christ to you in all His incomparable glory; and when this happens, you will certainly not be attracted by any other of the idols of the earth. "Christ in you, the hope of glory"—that is the Pauline prescription for a holy life. And we experience this as we allow the Holy Spirit in ungrieved sovereignty to control us.

A life of victory over temptation is the birthright of every Christian. It is also the birthright of every Christian couple. You must walk "in the light with one another." When you do, you will find that "the blood of Jesus will keep on cleansing you from every sin." This is victory. Claim it by faith for yourselves. God waits to honor the faith that will demand such absolute purity.

But more. Be compassionate to those who have gone out of the way. "Blessed are the merciful; they shall obtain mercy." It is very dangerous to adopt a posture of judgment on any of our fellows. "Be not high-minded; but fear." Who was it who first said—"There but for the grace of God go I"? It is not easy to turn homosexuals from their chosen path. But it is possible. Somewhere along the line they have missed knowing the fulness of the love of God in Christ. You may be able to tell them about Him and show that "He is able to save unto the uttermost all that come unto God by Him." This is our mission. Our homes, if they are wholly committed to Christ, may become rescue areas for sinners of deepest dye. Go out and help. Compel the wanderer to come in. Tell Him that "with God nothing is impossible." You will never regret it.

12: Contraception and Birth Control

What is birth control? I suppose we should start there.

Surely. Birth control is any practice designed to ensure that as a result of sexual intimacy there will be no reproduction. The quest for this has gone on from the first phases of civilization. How can you prevent the introduction of the male sperm to the female egg? Until recently, it has proved an almost impossible assignment, as the minute sperm cells carry within them an uncontrollable constraint to radar-in on the expectant egg. Every effort made to hinder their advance was usually circumvented and overcome.

The reason for wanting to prevent the sperm from meeting the egg is that when it happens pregnancy results, and pregnancy is often the last thing that two people having intercourse want. Numberless husbands and wives have had their sexual desires dulled and jaded by the recurrent worry that every act of intercourse might mean another mouth to feed. And, of course, where illicit intercourse is involved, the anxiety is all the greater to stop the possibility of conception.

What have been the methods used in the past? Or, what can you tell us of the history of birth control?

Contraceptive techniques were known in ancient civilizations and were practiced almost up to modern times without significant alteration. It was in England, however, that the first major movement towards birth control began. In the revised edition of his *Essay on the Principle of Population* (1803), Thomas Robert Malthus, economist, sociologist and pioneer in modern population studies, pressed for the preventive check of "moral restraint." His theories caused great controversy but were accepted by groups who called themselves the neo-Malthusians. In 1877, Annie Besant and Charles Bradlaugh were put on trial for selling *The Fruits of Philosophy*, a pamphlet written in 1832 by an American, Charles Knowlton; the pamphlet dealt with those contraceptive methods known and practiced at that time. After this famous trial, the Malthusian League was founded, and in 1878 the first birth-control clinic was opened in Amsterdam by Aletta Jacobs. In 1921, with the aid and support of Dr. Marie Stopes, the Malthusian League established a clinic for birth control—especially for poor mothers—in London. The first U.S. birth-control clinic was opened in 1916 by Margaret Sanger; her center was in Brooklyn, N.Y. This was closed by the police, and Mrs. Sanger received a thirty-day prison sentence. In 1923 a permanent clinic was opened by the League and similar ones were opened gradually at other points across the country. Between 1920 and 1960 a tremendous amount of pressure was brought to bear on legislators in the United States, and several federal and state laws were disallowed by the courts. At the time John F. Kennedy assumed the office of President, there were only two states, Massachusetts and Connecticut, that continued to enforce laws forbidding a doctor to offer contraceptive advice to a married woman patient. What this meant was that by the middle of the twentieth century, public acceptance of birth control in the United States and western Europe had become widespread. In 1958, the Lambeth Conference of Bishops of the Church of England still accepted a statement that strongly denounced any form of family planning through the use of contraceptives. But now, many countries—India especially, but also Egypt, China, Pakistan and Ceylon—have given high priority to birth control, and in India alone there are today nearly 10,000 control clinics together with a great number of sterilization centers. The "population explosion," a phrase that became current only in the sixties, is one of the major concerns of sociologists and politicians in our time.

Is there any official policy of the Churches of today?

Only in the Roman Catholic Church is birth control by contraceptives rigidly forbidden. In fact, Pope Paul has made himself highly unpopular by refusing to bow to the almost universal clamor within his church for a favorable restatement on the subject. The rhythm method of control is the only one officially allowed to Roman Catholics, and perhaps this is the place to state what this method is. Since fertilization is more likely to occur a day or two before or after ovulation, and since ovulation usually takes place about mid-point in the menstrual cycle—that is, about fourteen days before the next menstrual period is due—then, if intercourse is avoided at that time, there is much less likelihood of fertilization and pregnancy. But the method is not foolproof. For one thing, no woman can guarantee on exactly what day her next period will begin, and what's more, ovulation can actually happen on any day of the menstrual cycle, even during menstruation itself. The so-called "safe period" is pretty much of a delusion.

It is interesting to note that at the present time Roman Catholics in Great Britain are mounting a very strong protest campaign against the Pope's firm attitude. The same independence seems to be asserting itself in Canada and the United States. A spring 1970 poll of Roman Catholic mothers in the United States showed that a good 50 per cent of them were regularly using oral contraceptives, and one of the most prominent drug companies in Canada reports that the sale of oral contraceptives is almost identical in Ontario and Quebec. Quebec, of course, is devoutly Roman Catholic in the main.

Most major religious bodies other than the Roman Catholic Church have either officially accepted the intelligent use of contraceptives or have had this view stated by one of their commissions. Among Protestants it is generally left as a matter for the corporate conscience of husband and wife to decide.

What is the oral contraceptive like?

It is a small pill containing a chemical substance that prevents ovulation in women. The basic elements in the pill are an oestrogen compound and a progesterone derivative. Various formulas are presented by different drug companies. In some cases, pure oestrogen is taken for sixteen days, and then a combination of both elements for the last five. This is known as the sequential method. For this to be successful, women have to watch their calendars very closely. The first pill for the month must be taken on the fifth day after menstruation begins and not one day must be missed in the succeeding twenty-one.

Recently, the safety of the pill has been challenged for various reasons, particularly because of evidence that it contributes to blood clotting. Intensive research has been undertaken to ascertain what element in the pill causes this, and it appears that at least part of the problem has been a higher dosage of oestrogen than is necessary. Indeed, a reduction of 50 per cent in the amount formerly prescribed by some manufacturers has shown no diminishing of the effectiveness of the pill. The sequential pills are almost 100 per cent effective. Almost! One of the loveliest of children around our church at the present time came when the parents felt they were adequately ensured against pregnancy. But eventually, no doubt, a pill will be marketed that is altogether effective and carries no possibility of undesirable side effects. When that day comes, sexual intercourse may be indulged in without the slightest fear of further developments.

Is there any biblical argument against using the pill?

I do not think so. We have noted already that sexual intercourse as originally designed by God and given to men, has two quite distinct functions. One of them is procreative, the perpetuation of the human race through the conception, birth and rearing of children. The other, and this is quite a distinct function from that of procreation, is the binding together of two lives in the most intimate of human bonds, the bond of love. I have stressed from time to time that in any well-adjusted marriage there will always be found mutual satisfaction in intercourse with one another. The unitive factor of husband and wife in intercourse with each other is as important as any other factor.

Now if by intercourse there is always the possibility of pregnancy, the totality of the human race could very soon reach astronomical proportions. But this is not God's plan. Moreover, the size of a family ought to accord with the financial resources of the parents and, in fact, with their own wishes. One way to prevent procreation, of course, is to abstain from sexual intercourse. Some deliberately choose this road. I personally think it is an unfortunate choice, especially since modern medical science has produced alternatives. There is, to be sure, a fundamental issue involved in taking the pill, and it is an issue that husband and wife should firmly agree on. We are discussing the situation between a husband and wife and nothing else at the moment. No one really knows to what extent the discovery of the pill has made sexual promiscuity easier and more extensive. We are not discussing that question now. What we are asking is this: Is there any basic reason why a Christian man and woman, determined to be the best for God, and eager to have only the family that He intends they should have, should not use the pill? My answer is that I can see no reason why this should not be done. It can make family planning so much easier. It can take from the experience of sexual intercourse a thousand fears that otherwise might blight and darken the togetherness of wife and husband. My counsel is that, under a physician's careful prescribing, no one should hesitate to use it for the highest and noblest ends.

Are there other factors we should note about the pill?

Possibly. This is of course a vast subject, and we could easily slide away from the main intent of this book, which is to give the most practical and Christian counselling on all matters that relate to sex and marriage. But this can be said at least. It is still too early to determine what long-range effects the widespread use of this contraceptive will have on the whole area of intimacies in marriage. The wife is robbed by it of the most natural of reasons for not having intercourse if she doesn't wish it at a given time. Studies are being made in many places on such questions as, "Is there any evidence that the husband becomes less interested in intercourse after his wife has been on the pill for an extended time?" and, alternatively, "Is there any evidence that a woman loses her desire for intercourse after an extended time on the pill?" The next ten years will see an ever spreading stream of studies in this field, both medical and psychological. We must wait and see.

There is no doubt, however, that the pill is the most revolutionary discovery of the twentieth century in the area of sex and marriage relationships.

What other forms of contraception are there?

For those who are unwilling to use the pill for any reason probably the most commonly used method of contraception is the simple douche. This is a straightforward washing out of the vaginal passage after intercourse has taken place. Various douche compounds are on the market, and they can be obtained from any drug store. Water is of course the primary ingredient, and water used without any additive may be as effective as anything else. The patented types you see on the shelves of drug stores are usually better in their looks than in their effectiveness. They come as compounds of chlorophyll or mercury; some even contain carbolic acid. To have any hope of effectiveness, it is absolutely essential to act immediately, and you must do a really thorough job if you hope to clear the sperm away. But you can never be sure. Carbolic acid is even dangerous. Avoid it.

"Coitus interruptus" should be mentioned. This is simply removing the penis from the vagina immediately prior to the moment of discharge. Many women, in talking with their doctor, say that "their husbands are very careful." This is what they usually mean. I have read estimates somewhere that possibly 50 per cent of all sexual intercourse ends in this way. But it is by no means a good method. For one thing, in the initial stages of penis-contacting-vagina there is a secretion of sperm which may prove perfectly effective in supplying all that is needed by an awaiting ovum in the woman. In addition, it is really a denial of the true sexual act, giving release in some sense to the husband but doing very little for the wife; and, as I have been ceaselessly stressing, the whole objective of the sexual intercourse is to bind husband and wife together more closely than ever before. Where this is a problem, it would be advisable to discuss the matter together with your physician. He will have lots of ideas on the question of timing, rhythm, and adjustment to each other's needs. This method is certainly not to be commended.

What else?

A most useful contraceptive and one that is being increasingly used is what is called simply "foam." This contraceptive is amazingly effective. Where the pill is virtually 100 per cent foolproof, contraceptive foam has demonstrated a pregnancy rate of only 2.7 per cent. In other words, it is 97.3 per cent effective. There is no doubt that this is the best alternative to the pill so far as effectiveness goes. The rhythm method is highly variable, allowing anything from a 15 to a 35 per cent rate of pregnancy. Foam is very simple to use. It is injected into the vagina before each act of intercourse through an applicator that comes with the purchase.

Is there any kind of pill for men?

Unfortunately, no. But tremendous research is being undertaken in this field and it is highly probable that in the near future some such product may be discovered. It is too bad that the onus falls so heavily on the woman in her quest for adequate protection against conception. The male can of course undergo a simple operation known as vasectomy—which we will discuss later—and once this has happened, the wife is immediately freed from all fear of unwanted pregnancy. Interest in this is increasing in our Western world. I know a number of couples who, feeling that they now have as many children as they can adequately care for, are seriously studying this possibility. I know some men who have had it done. But husband and wife must be fully persuaded in their own minds and jointly that this is the right thing to do. If this is so, go right ahead. There is very little doubt but that you will be glad you did.

What about mechanical devices?

Yes, this must be mentioned. The vaginal diaphragm was possibly the most popular form of birth control in the North American continent prior to the appearance of the pill. Many physicians would still make it their first choice. The diaphragm is a flexible rubber disk placed in the vagina immediately at the spot where the vagina opens into the womb. This spot is known as the cervix. The objective of this protective covering is to ensure that no sperm enters the womb. It is a physician's job to fit a diaphragm properly; the size of the vaginal passage differs from woman to woman, and it is therefore essential that the right size of covering be used. Once the diaphragm has been fitted by the physician, he should then teach the woman how to insert it into position for maximum effect. If properly placed, there will be no sensation of the diaphragm's presence by either husband or wife during intercourse. The diaphragm should be held tightly in position with the aid of vaginal jelly—a jelly which contains a chemical that kills sperm on contact. Since rubber is waterproof and assumedly sperm-proof, the diaphragm should be completely effective. But it is hard to find perfection in our world; and unless it is placed on the exact spot, and held firmly there during the turbulence and agitation of copulation, it may become a gateway to millions of life-germs through the cervix.

Nonetheless, it has for a long time been in constant use in countless homes; and the results have in many cases been good. There is the advantage with this instrument that it can be set in position some time before sexual intercourse takes place. After intercourse, the diaphragm and jelly should be left in position for at least ten hours. Then the vagina should be washed out thoroughly and, if everything has been in position, all should be well.

Then there is the condom, which is a protective covering over the penis. It is known by many names, including rubber, safety, and cundum. Originally, condoms were fashioned from fine linen fitting loosely over the penis. Then fish bladder and lamb gut were used. But they were really more of a nuisance than a help. The latest models are of the finest latex rubber, which gives a skin-tight fit over the penis. They should never be used without a liberal supply of vaginal jelly. This is first inserted into the vagina near the mouth of the womb and deposited there with the aid of a plastic applicator—again, all part of the package you can buy at your corner drugstore. Some of the jelly should also be used at the inside point of the condom in order to help it flex and stretch instead of binding. The rest of the condom should cover the penis completely, being lubricated with the vaginal jelly over the top two-thirds at least. If this is done, there should be no possibility of its slipping off during intercourse. Great care should be taken to ensure that after intercourse, the condom is abstracted intact from the vagina.

It is customary to use the condom on only one occasion. If for any reason, financial or otherwise, it is necessary to use a condom more than once, it should be minutely examined for cracks or pinholes which could negate the whole objective of the procedure. Normally, when once used, discard.

Is the condom a safe method? Mostly. The Advisory Committee on Obstetrics and Gynecology of the U.S. Food and Drug Administration gives it a rating of about 85 per cent. The advantages of the condom are that it is inexpensive, simple, easily available, speedy and discardable. It has the further advantage of providing some protection against venereal disease. And that is an all-important matter.

By using the condom method, the husband takes a large measure of responsibility from his wife in the effort to prevent conception. This is undoubtedly appreciated by the wife far more than many men realize. But a 15 per cent possibility of conception is high when compared with the almost 100 per cent security of the pill and the 97 per cent of contraceptive foam. Only you can choose.

Can you say something more about sterilization?

In the case of men, the procedure is known as a vasectomy. This operation is very simple and can be completed within half an hour in a doctor's office. As we have already noted, the tube that leads from the testicle to the penis is known as the vas deferens. If this canal is sealed off, sperm can no longer be introduced into the seminal fluid and thus will not be ejaculated at orgasm. This is a very decisive form of birth control, and is very common in India, where the government actually offers a small sum of money (or occasionally a small transistor radio) to men who undergo the operation. The government of India has become increasingly concerned about the population explosion and has been encouraging every method of curbing it. One of the best known buildings in all of India is the building in which birth-control techniques are taught and treatments given.

I should, however, hasten to add that the vasectomy is becoming much more common on this continent. This is part of the widening process of sex education. Men know that this is possible today. And if they are concerned to take the load of responsibility from their wives' shoulders, then this affords a ready means of response. I have no figures, but I am assured by several authorities with whom I have spoken that it is definitely on the increase. The motivation for this can be only good.

A note of warning should be added here. Recently a friend of mine dropped in to see me. He wanted to share something very special. It was this. He had accepted the procedure of vasectomy and had felt that this irrevocably meant no more children for him or his wife. But no! Within a month his wife was pregnant. His doctor had not told him that living sperm can thrive in the duct for about six weeks after the vasectomy. Such sperm should be flushed out by ejaculations over that period of time.

There is a similar operation for women?

Yes, a woman too may be sterilized absolutely. One way is by tubal ligation, which means cutting and tying the fallopian tubes. When this is done, there is of course no way for the egg to reach the sperm or the sperm the egg. They are sealed off from each other. A woman can also undergo a complete hysterectomy, which is the removal of the uterus. This is not prescribed except where there are other factors prompting it. But whatever the procedure for women, it is never as easy as it is for men. The procedure is accompanied with considerable discomfort and pain.

Have we discussed all the birth-control methods?

Not yet! What is known as the Intra-Uterine Device, or IUD for short, has been around for a long time. Aristotle refers to it–and that's going back almost 2500 years. More recently, a German doctor, Ernst Grafenberg by name, revived the method, fashioning a coil of silver wire that was then inserted through the vagina into the uterus. The pregnancy rate dropped dramatically. Later, he introduced several refinements of his method, but the basic principle remained the same.

Unfortunately, though he argued his thesis intensely and widely, he was equally intensely attacked by medical authorities in many lands. The result was that the IUD was for a long time given up as a lost cause. It wasn't until the early 1950s that an Israeli physician, Lazar Margulies, reintroduced the method, but with a different substance–polyethylene plastic for silver wire. The body apparently tolerates plastic better than silver. But there are some women who cannot tolerate even a plastic device. Vaginal bleeding may occur, or general pelvic discomfort. The woman's body may even expel the device, though this is quite unusual.

How does the loop—which once placed in the uterus is meant to stay there—compare with other means of contraception? Exceptionally well. The performance rate is really excellent—almost 95 per cent effective. In countries that are still backward in many ways, the loop may well be the method of choice. But with the advent of the pill, it would appear as though its days are numbered. We must wait and see.

When is the best time for a couple to discuss birth control?

The earlier the better. It is clearly wise for a couple intending marriage to discuss the whole question of having a family, and that means discussing family planning. Christian young people should be fully informed about all methods of birth control. If modern medical science has placed in our hands tools that our forefathers did not have, we should thank God for them and ask His will as to how we should use them. It is beyond question that we live in an entirely different world from that of a century ago, and we would not be fulfilling our true duty to God and to one another if we did not acquaint ourselves with all the options that lie open to us. Obviously, if one or both of the partners are Roman Catholic and have any conscientious scruples about disobeying the fiat of the Church, the whole issue of birth control should be discussed very early in the engagement.

Unfortunately, there are cases where pregnancy does not occur in spite of the most ardent wish of both husband and wife. If this condition continues for an extended period, you should consult your doctor to see if there is any way in which help can be given. There may be some very simple part of the machinery that is not functioning or functioning properly. In the last resort, of course, children are "a heritage of the Lord." It is God alone who can grant the gift of childbearing to any woman. Therefore you should, above all other considerations, see to it that God is remembered and that you commit all your ways to Him. The words of the prophet Isaiah are worth keeping in mind:

> I will wait upon the Lord, that hideth His face from the

> house of Jacob, and I will look for Him. Behold, I and the children whom the Lord hath given me are for signs and wonders in Israel from the Lord of hosts, which dwelleth in Mount Zion (Isaiah 8:17, 18).

This is where your case ultimately rests. God gives. God withholds. The prayer of Hannah should be the prayer of every Christian wife:

> She vowed a vow and said, "O Lord of hosts, if Thou wilt indeed look on the affliction of thine handmaid, and remember me, and not forget thy handmaid, but wilt give unto thine handmaid a man child, then I will give him unto the Lord all the days of his life" (I Samuel 1:11).

In answer to this prayer Samuel was born. And Hannah was true to her promise. She gave over her son to the service of God from his earliest years. Praying mothers make great men. We need many more Hannahs in the Church today. Certainly, whatever children the Lord gives you, pray for them. You can do nothing greater for them.

13: Abortion

I'm almost afraid to ask this question but I must. Do you think that there is any place for therapeutic abortion in the thoughts of Christian parents?

Well, I'm glad you have raised the question, for it is a vital one. We cannot avoid it, especially in days when governments in many parts of the world are liberalizing the laws concerning therapeutic abortion.

Let's be clear about our definitions. An abortion is the expulsion of the human foetus before it has attained independent viability, that is, before it is able to survive outside the mother's womb. This is commonly taken to be within the first twenty-eight weeks. It should be understood that a mother may abort naturally and very much against her will. Normally this is called a miscarriage. A therapeutic abortion, on the other hand, is definitely enacted by design and with medical help; it is the deliberate ending of pregnancy, the deliberate termination of the growth of the foetus within the womb of the mother.

Is there any normal reason for spontaneous abortion? Or, if I may put it in another way, What is the usual cause of miscarriage?

Many factors enter into this. There may be some natural defect in the mother. I think of a young wife who lost a baby in the third month of pregnancy. She has only one kidney; and while a perfectly normal life may be lived by anyone with one kidney, the strain of producing another life with one kidney may prove too great. This is the reason assumed for her spontaneous abortion. She became pregnant again, however, and this time, under intensive care, she carried her baby successfully and gave birth to a lovely daughter.

There is always the possibility that there may be some defect in the sperm or the egg, with the result that an imperfect product is on the way from the beginning. When the body rejects this imperfect embryo, it is in actual fact fulfilling a very great service both to the parents and to society in general. There is little doubt that the birth would be that of a deformed child. Babies with two heads, babies without heads, babies with heads but no brains, babies with hollow brains bursting right through their skulls: these are some of the features that arise from an imperfect ovum or sperm. It is really a benevolent nature that casts off such before they reach the period of normal birth. While miscarriage of this sort may cause much sorrow and disappointment to the parents at the time of its occurrence, it may well be that they have been saved from great sorrow in days to come. This can happen to any mother. Genetic mistakes or misfits regard neither time nor place nor rank. A Christian couple must simply commit everything to the care and control of an all-wise God who knows the end from the beginning.

But not all miscarriages show evidence of malformation of the foetus. They can occur through some malfunction of the female reproductive organs at a given point in time. It may be at the critical moment when the fertilized egg is being attached to the wall of the womb. At that point it is always possible that the circulatory system of the mother does not properly connect to the baby's blood supply. The result? Spontaneous abortion.

What is the frequency-rate of such spontaneous abortions?

About 10 per cent to 15 per cent of all pregnancies. That is a high percentage and some authorities give an even higher figure. Usually, of course, the foetus has died before it is expelled by the mother's bodily mechanism. Spontaneous abortions of this kind can be exceedingly painful, though the mother usually recovers quickly. What has to be stressed at this point is that there are many mothers with large families who have suffered miscarriage in earlier years. Should miscarriage ever happen to you, be sure to get the best possible medical counsel. There may be some natural deficiency in your blood that can easily be rectified. There are many maternal dysfunctions that predispose to abortion. Let these be searched out thoroughly by the most competent medical minds you can obtain. Then leave the rest with God. At the heart of the Christian faith is the tremendous truth of the sovereignty and providence of God. "All things work together for good to them that love God, to them that are called according to His purpose" (Romans 8:28).

> Judge not the Lord by feeble sense,
> But trust Him for His grace;
> Behind a frowning providence
> He hides a smiling face.

In acceptance of God's will you discover peace. He will never allow anything to happen that is not for your good and His highest glory.

But what about therapeutic abortion? Is there any place for this in the Christian mind?

This, of course, is a different question entirely. Recently, there have been some very significant changes in the attitudes of governments on this subject, and this cannot fail to complicate the thinking of the Christian. But we must face the question openly and unafraid.

The answer of the Roman Catholic Church is unequivocal. Abortion is always wrong. In 1588 Pope Sixtus V declared that the soul entered the embryo at the moment of conception. Pope Gregory XIV who followed him altered that dictate; but in 1869 Pope Pius IX reaffirmed the position of Sixtus, and so it remains to this day. "She conceived and brought forth." The plain meaning of this, according to the Roman Catholic Church, is that at the moment of conception, life is implanted. To terminate such pregnancy by any artificial means is in reality murder. It is the deliberate taking of life, and God has said: "Thou shalt not kill."

In the ancient world other views were held. In ancient Greece, procreation was forbidden without state sanction and this made abortion mandatory, at least in many cases. Aristotle defended abortion on the ground that the rational soul entered the embryo only at an advanced point of development. In his view, the child-to-be was endowed at conception with the principle of vegetative life only, exchanged after some days with animal life, and only after the passage of time and at a much later state with a rational soul. Roman law went even further, holding that the human person begins to exist only at birth. Under such conditions, abortion was naturally very easy.

Does the Bible discuss this at all?

It is difficult to believe that David did not believe in soul-conception even within the womb of the mother. Consider Psalm 139 from verse 14 onwards:

> I will praise Thee: for I am fearfully and wonderfully made: marvellous are Thy works: and that my soul knoweth right well.
>
> My substance was not hid from Thee, when I was made in secret, and curiously wrought in the lowest parts of the earth.
>
> Thine eyes did see my substance, yet being unperfect; and in Thy book all my members were written, which in continuance were fashioned, when as yet there was none of them.
>
> How precious also are Thy thoughts to me, O God; how great is the sum of them!

Now here is a biblical position. David declares clearly that the creation of the foetus is one of the wonderful works of God. This is among the sublimest miracles of His creative power. And God knows all our members even when they are still "unperfect." Can one easily turn from a passage like this and accept the modern humanistic position that is so often advanced—namely, that the foetus is without rights if the mother for any reason whatsoever says so? One can very easily reach a position of infanticide even though the real act may be only that of twentieth-century feticide.

It must nevertheless be conceded that the Bible does not discuss abortion in any specific way. Equally, at no point does the Bible discuss our modern methods for the treatment of diabetes or the latest types of surgery used for the rehabilitation of lepers. On both of these latter areas there have been tremendous advances; and had such modern techniques been available during Mosaic times, we can be sure that this knowledge would have been widely disseminated and put to the best use. The silence of the Bible on the issue of therapeutic abortion is not in itself an absolute denial of its possibility and propriety.

A well-known phrase from the Westminster Confession of Faith might well be quoted here. After declaring that in the Holy Scriptures we have "the infallible truth and divine authority" of the Word of God made clear to us through "the inward work of the Holy Spirit" (Chap. 1:5), the Confession goes on to state boldly that "The whole counsel of God, concerning all things necessary for his own glory, man's salvation, faith, and life, is either expressly set down in Scripture, or by good and necessary consequence may be adduced from Scripture." This phrase "by good and necessary consequence" must be kept in mind when we discuss such an issue as therapeutic abortion. The Bible is not like an encyclopedia to which you can turn for an explicit answer to any question that may confront you. On the contrary, in many areas of life we have to deduce what is right from the *principles* that are clearly enunciated in the Bible. Therapeutic abortion may be such a case. This subject itself is not discussed in Scripture. But one should ask if there are guiding principles that can provide a lead.

One would urge caution in using this phrase "by good and necessary consequence" in the case of abortion. It may be true that we can now tell at the twelfth week of pregnancy whether a defective little life is going to be born—it is possible now to determine at that stage whether the child will be mongoloid or not—but can you thereby automatically determine whether this life should come to birth? Much of the argument for eugenic abortion rests on this principle. But in the last analysis it must be conceded that there is no absolute Scriptural warrant for the practice.

What do you mean when you speak of "eugenic abortion"?

A eugenic abortion is an abortion undertaken to prevent the birth of what will certainly be a seriously defective child.

In the abortion debate, how much weight should be given to foetal abnormalities? As we have already noted, it is now possible to tell prospective parents whether their child will be mongoloid or not. In the interest of eugenics, should this birth be aborted? And what about evidence of other irremediable abnormalities?

This is an agonizing dilemma for many parents today. Take the case of a pregnant mother who contracts German measles or rubella. In children, German measles is a slight virus disease. Most children contract it at some time in their youth. They are sick for a week and then they get better, with no ill effects. But if a pregnant mother contracts it, the consequences may be dire. It works somehow like this. If the mother succumbs to German measles in the first four weeks of pregnancy, the chances of her giving birth to a deformed child are 50 per cent; in the fourth to the eighth week, 25 per cent; and from the eighth to the twelfth week, 17 per cent. Suppose this happens to a Christian mother in about the seventh week of pregnancy. She stands a fifty-fifty chance of producing a deformed child. What do you then advise in such a situation? What is right? My counsel in such cases is that the parents make this a matter of intense prayer and that they ask their friends to pray for them. I believe that God will make His will known to them if they truly seek it. The guidance given may be to allow the pregnancy to continue, and ultimately a child may be born blind or deaf or having a diseased heart or a retarded mind. But he will enter a circle of love that will never forsake him. On the other hand, if a deep sense of compulsion grows in the minds of both parents that it would be wrong to allow the pregnancy to continue, commit the matter entirely into the care of God and secure the best doctor you can find to carry the necessary abortion procedure through. Friends may criticize, censure and blame you. Never mind. You must be persuaded in your own mind and do what you deem to be right. Leave the ultimate judgment with God.

This means that you do accept the principle of therapeutic abortion?

Yes! But only under the most stringent rules. A mother may suffer a nervous breakdown during pregnancy and as a direct result of it. This may be uncommon, but it does occur. In cases like this, the only resort may be abortion. If abortion is necessary to save the life of the mother, then the choice is comparatively easy. But even here, there are many sections of the Christian community who would have very strong reservations. It is wrong to dogmatize. The problem has become all the greater for many by virtue of the fact that state laws have greatly liberalized the rules covering abortion. Furthermore, one must ask the question whether Christians should try to influence public policy. Quite frequently, powerful religious pressure groups have exerted political power to impede the liberalization of laws on divorce, contraception, homosexuality and abortion. There is nothing wrong in this. On questions that relate to the welfare of men, a citizen is both privileged and obligated to make such decisions as he deems to be best for the greatest possible number. When a person is a Christian, this responsibility increases. And this clearly indicates that not only should a Christian try to discover for himself what the principles of Scripture are regarding abortion, but he must also rally support from both Christian and non-Christian groups when he believes that the welfare of humanity is the point at issue.

Who should have the last word in the process of decision-making?

The prospective parents. They will do so naturally after securing the very best advice. That advice should come from the doctor, a pastor, a lawyer, and such other advisers as there may be. But in the last analysis, the decision is a lonely one, and often made after days of agonizing indecision.

State laws must of course be known. You must discover what is legal in the place where you live. A very interesting situation has arisen in Canada. The Criminal Code was amended in 1968, and under the new laws, abortion has been made legal when a panel of at least three doctors, one of whom must be a psychiatrist, has given unanimous consent that a therapeutic abortion is desirable. Now that may seem very equitable, just and right. But the outworking of the law has produced inequities that were never foreseen by the legislators. Men are men and opinions vary. *Quot homines, tot sententiae.* In one large city, 50 per cent of all pregnancies in a certain hospital are being aborted. It is a large hospital with a large number of beds, and it is staffed by young, eager and open-minded doctors. The panel of at least three can easily be found to give consent. Elsewhere, some hospitals haven't so many beds, and the number of procedures there is much fewer.

Uniformity was expected under the new law. But it simply isn't turning out that way. What has happened is that those most eager to secure abortion go to the hospitals where they are most readily obtained. The law has been altered and therapeutic abortion has been made much easier to obtain. But a human factor is left, and it seems that there are many variants because of this. As we have indicated, the final word must be with the prospective parents. But the physician who knows the patient best should be authorized to go ahead without delay if he concurs. If he does not concur, he should explain most fully the medical, moral or psychological reasons, or any combination of these, why he does not want to proceed.

Is there any evidence from countries or states that have had liberal abortion laws for some considerable time?

This is a very interesting question. Roumania, after ten years of liberalization, returned in 1966 to a more restrictive law. The government there found evidence that unrestricted abortion carried serious long-term implications. The birth rate had dropped alarmingly from 24.2 to 14.3 per 1,000 inhabitants, and medical authorities began to question the uncertain effects on women's health. Soviet medical authorities, according to Daniel Callahan in *Abortion; Law, Choice and Morality,* are generally agreed that "widespread abortion, even legal abortion, still remains a sufficient hazard to a woman's health to warrant being discouraged." Yugoslav health workers are told to "regard abortion as biologically, medically, psychologically, and sociologically harmful." Callahan stresses that in eastern Europe, where there has been considerable experimentation in this whole area, "there is nothing in any published writings to indicate that abortion should be removed from any kind of legal control." There is also evidence that the 1967 Colorado law has produced serious disillusionment because it has not significantly lowered the number of illegal abortions. The evidence to date from lands that have had some extended experience is that the liberalizing of abortion laws is no clear pass to a better and more wholesome society.

Is the surgical procedure simple or very serious?

Quite simple if the pregnancy is under twelve weeks. The opening to the womb is called the cervix. It is a narrow opening and during pregnancy has been hermetically sealed. In order to procure abortion, the cervix is dilated by a special surgical instrument, and then, either with a suction machine or a sharp curette (a broad smooth loop of surgical steel with an extended handle), the surgeon dislodges the embryo from the wall of the womb. By long experience he knows when this has been done. Some bleeding may occur, but it is easily controlled by medication. In a short time the woman can go home, and in a very few days everything is normal once more. The procedure is carried through under anaesthetic, and there is very little discomfort.

I have a question of a different kind. Suppose there is no danger to the mother's health, but the addition of another mouth to feed is going to make the family dip over the poverty line, would this not be a strong argument for therapeutic abortion, especially if the pregnancy results from the incontinence of the husband?

This is a very vital question. I have met with it repeatedly. I have seen the despair in many a mother's eyes as she has realized that once again she is pregnant and she knows that it has been almost impossible to make ends meet in the past. An extra mouth to feed may well make the difference between self-respect and abject poverty. It is hard to advise. Most doctors would, I believe, be ready to grant release from the burden of childbearing on this score, the ground being that the mother's health is going to be affected in coming days if not immediately. On the other hand, one has to think of large families in the past that have been raised on a shoestring budget and yet ultimately have proved very great blessings to the world. One need mention only the Wesleys. I find it impossible in situations like this to give advice. Only the mother and her doctor can guide. To any Christian who finds himself in such a position, I can only say this: You must cast the matter upon the Lord. You must await His clear direction. It is very easy to be critical of another's incontinence or of the unwillingness of a father to undergo the very simple surgical procedure that would make such a situation an impossibility. In many cases, men just don't know that such facilities exist. In other cases, they are simply inconsiderate. To condemn a family, however, to live permanently under the poverty line is a bitter prescription and does not seem very ethical. But is abortion God's answer?

Are abortions mainly sought for medical reasons?

If we are absolutely candid, I think we must readily admit that the answer to this question is No.

Social rationalization, personal and private preference, along with an element of antagonism to a code of ethics that makes abortion appear distasteful and wrong—these are far more frequently the reasons for abortion than purely medical reasons. Few would question the validity of abortion following rape or incest. Some years ago in England, a very prominent obstetrician placed his professional status and everything else on the line when he openly defied the law and procured an abortion for a raped girl. I had then, and still have, nothing but admiration for the stand this doctor took. In my eyes there was certainly no true intercourse between consenting adults. The initial act was a crime. To permit the pregnancy to continue would have compounded the crime.

One must also constantly test the validity of the options that face parents who may expect a deformed or defective child. In the context of Christian ethics, a decision regarding the termination of a seriously defective foetus is not easy. Too many persons with congenital deformities have subsequently been grateful for life, and too many parents have lovingly accepted a seriously defective child to allow us to classify abortion-for-abnormalities as a purely medical decision. We have already examined this in some detail. But we must emphasize that any dictum which simply avers that prenatal life is pre-human and therefore may be terminated arbitrarily is much too simplistic. Even if life in the womb is not life as it exists after delivery, there are still many cogent reasons for considering it human life in some form. We now know that the foetus receives its total genetic potential of RNA and DNA at the moment of conception. Since it is a unique and unrepeatable combination of proteins, it is surely in some sense alive. Furthermore, it should be stressed that by the end of four weeks a budding cardiovascular system is beginning to function in the foetus. Also extraordinary is that at eight weeks the electrical activity of the fetal brain is already readable, and except for limbs, all essential organ formations are present. The foetus is capable of spontaneous motion at ten weeks, and it responds to external stimuli before that. Surely, then, this question is in order: If breath of life and brain activity are important factors in determining the point of death, should not the same considerations determine the point of life's beginnings?

What do you say to anyone who has procured an abortion but is pursued with a deep sense of guilt?

I would hope to speak with such a person before the abortion is procured, for I am certain that feelings of guilt would be present then also. It is a fact that in spite of all the modern contraceptive know-how, there are many unwanted pregnancies. The ages at which pre-marital intercourse is accepted and at which undesired pregnancies occur are dropping lower and lower. In a host of such cases there is a terrifying sense of guilt.

What do I say? It is never easy to know what to say. It is certainly wrong to pretend that there are no moral issues involved. It is certainly unethical to try to make it appear that the whole affair is of little account. As a Christian pastor I speak of the sanctity of human life and of the stringent safeguards that God has laid down for the protection of all human life. At the same time, when pregnancy has occurred outside of marriage, I tell the prospective mother of the possibilities that exist for the birth of the baby, of the possibilities thereafter of adoption, and of the difficulties involved in trying to rear the child herself. I tell her also that "with the Lord there is mercy and abundant redemption" and that He can and will deal with her sense of guilt through the depths of His forgiveness and grace.

I recall an incident which I often relate to those faced with this traumatic ordeal. I once became acquainted with a girl who worked through an entire university year while her baby grew in her womb. She had left home where everybody knew what everyone else was doing, and she had come to the city to hide. In the providence of God she was taken into the heart of a wonderful Christian family. From that home she went to the hospital, and it was to this home that she returned after the birth—but without the baby. She found it hard to give him up. But she did.

And in the most unusual way I subsequently discovered where the baby was—now a boy full of life and health and ten years old. The home into which he had been guided by God was another equally wonderful Christian home. I felt that in all things God had worked together for good for everybody. This whole case had been made a matter of unceasing prayer. God surely answered the prayer we offered.

All you have said thus far refers to Christians. How do you advise non-Christians?

In the very same way. It is not really true to say that all I have been saying is for Christians only. I have been thinking of all sorts and classes of people. But when non-Christians do come and ask for counsel, I have often found that an occasion for witnessing to my own personal faith in Christ and of showing how relevant His Word is to situations such as they are in. Naturally I have met many girls who are pregnant and unmarried. They come and ask if I counsel marriage. Frequently I don't. Marriage is very often the worst possible answer to the problem. Every case is different. I try to show both the girl and the boy what they have missed by not belonging to Christ, and sometimes it has been possible to lead them to the Saviour. Not always, however. All I can do as a Christian is tell them what the Christian ethic is; remind them of the infinite sanctity of human life; tell them what the options are—including abortion; and pray with them, trusting that God will lead them aright. Invariably I make it clear that to choose abortion is an option that carries no guarantee of God's favor and blessing.

What is the connection between sexual promiscuity and more liberal abortion laws?

Do you mean does sexual promiscuity make abortion a more frequent choice of pregnant women? Or are you asking whether there is some kind of numerical ratio that can be pointed to as a standard of behavior?

The answer to the former is clearly Yes. Where there is promiscuity, unwanted pregnancies readily occur and therapeutic abortion becomes thereby a matter of strong desire. So far as the latter question is concerned, it is common judgment that while married women seeking therapeutic abortion once outnumbered unwed girls by four to one, the ratio is now almost equally balanced. It is the responsibility of the Christian, facing a society in which sexual libertinism is rife—"the sexual wilderness" as Vance Packard calls it—to stress such great biblical imperatives as "Abstain from fleshly lusts which war against the soul" (I Peter 2:11). It is the "pure in heart" who see God. The seed dies to live, the bread must be cast upon the waters, he that loses his life will save it. Union with God is by definition a continuous self-abandonment, a surrender of self. This is the life of those who see God and rejoice in that beatific vision. They are "pure in heart." And being thus pure, they long to see that purity manifested in every realm of their being and personality. Sexual promiscuity has no place in the life of a truly "pure" Christian man or maiden.

Any further counsel?

Well, of course, there are many areas of the subject that we haven't yet looked at. But we have covered the main points. I only hope and pray that it will never become necessary for you to take the route of abortion. But should this happen to you, pray for the heavenly ability to trust God absolutely. Should direct guidance be withheld from you, perhaps you should just leave the whole matter in God's hands and await His will. God is never a disappointment. I certainly know of cases where a retarded child has been a very great blessing to a home; and should this home ever be yours, then take it from the Lord whose "eye seeth every precious thing." Marriage and sex for all Christians demand that we face issues like these and know what are the pros and cons on the subject. Whatever else you do, never let your faith in God fail. "Children are a heritage of the Lord; and the fruit of the womb is His reward." If the fruit of the womb be imperfect, it will provide you another opportunity of manifesting the infinite love of God, your Saviour. In this way, you will demonstrate to everyone the wonder of His love and the "exceeding greatness of His power to usward."

Faint not, nor fear; His arm is near;
He changes not, and thou art dear;
Only believe and thou shalt see
That Christ is all in all to thee.

In ancient Rome, when fathers commonly wanted baby girls to die, they would leave them on public garbage heaps. This practice was sharply reproved by the early Christians. And they carried this belief back to the prenatal stage of life. Tertullian writes: "To hinder a birth is merely a speedier man-killing; nor does it matter whether you take away a life that is born, or destroy one that is coming to the birth. That is a man which is going to be one; you have the fruit already in the seed." And in *The Apostolic Constitution,* a Christian document which comes from the fourth century, it is written: "Thou shalt not slay the child by causing abortion, nor kill that which is begotten; for everything that is shaped, and has received a soul from God, if it be slain, shall be avenged as being unjustly destroyed."

These are solemn words with which to end this chapter. They should be kept in mind as you read and re-read this whole section. Certainly, we should remember that part of the inheritance of being made "in the image of God" is the power of creativity, and especially the power to bring human life to birth. Great is our privilege. Great is our responsibility.

14: Venereal Disease

What is the origin of the name venereal?

That's a good question to ask. Venus was in the ancient world the goddess of love. The association becomes plain when you see this. Not that the association is appropriate—far from it. Disease is not a gift you give to a loved one if you can help it. But since the diseases covered under the name of venereal disease are all contracted through sexual contact—which in its highest form is an expression of love between two lovers—the reason for the name is clear.

Are there many types of venereal disease?

Five principal diseases, though three of them you may scarcely have heard about; the other two are well known. Let me talk first of all about the lesser-known ones. You will realize, of course, that in introducing this chapter into a book that is meant for all Christians, I sincerely hope that there is no Christian reading these pages who has in any way suffered or is suffering from these loathsome diseases. It should be understood very definitely that there is no other way of contracting them than by having sexual intercourse with one who is already afflicted. It is the responsibility of any doctor to report every case of such diseases to the health officer of his community. When this has been done, every effort is made to reach back to the contact whence the trouble has spread. There is no reason at all why these diseases should not be rooted out completely. We have the necessary drugs to kill them, indeed to overkill them. Yet, unfortunately, the rate of growth is rising steadily. According to the American Medical Association, venereal disease of all kinds increased by 200 per cent between 1960 and 1965. Alarming? When you know what the disease is like and some of its effects, it's more than alarming!

What are the three that are least well known?

You may have difficulty in remembering them. But for the sake of the record it is good to have them noted here.

Chancroid is one. It is possibly the least serious of these three evils but is a most distasteful kind of illness. It is caused by the presence of bacteria under the skin in the area of the genitals. Blisters form filled with pus. Very quickly the blisters break out into sore ulcers, and the ulcers spread right across the genital region. There are two forms of attack. One type gets deep under the skin, and in men may burst through the penis into the urethra causing urine to leak uncontrollably. The other form spreads rapidly across the thighs and stomach.

Once diagnosed accurately, there is effective treatment for this disease. The sulfa drugs have proved very effective here. But the trouble is in the diagnosis. Since the trouble is still relatively uncommon in the Western world, there hasn't been the necessary research on it to ensure speedy and accurate awareness of the disease. This disease is usually localized and self-limiting; but it can be most painful and disabling.

The second of the lesser-known venereal diseases is granuloma inguinale. Like chancroid, it is caused by bacteria. The genitals begin to show little bumps which gradually turn into leaking gobs of tissue and spread across the penis, the labia, the clitoris and the anus. Occasionally, some parts of the genital area will enlarge enormously. Sometimes, if the problem is not treated, the patient gradually withers away and dies. This can be a killer disease. There are major problems associated with it. One of these is the long period of gestation of the bacteria—at least three months; and since the first signs of the trouble are relatively painless, it is possible for the sufferer to avoid treatment expecting the symptoms to disappear. The proper treatment is streptomycin and the tetracycline drugs.

Third among these lesser-known but dread diseases is lymphogranuloma venereum, or LGV for short. Two or three weeks after exposure, there appears a small button-like rising in the sexual organs. This is followed after another fortnight by a bump as large as an egg. The trouble is by now well established. Whereas the former two diseases are bacterial in basis, this trouble arises from a virus infection. Another difference is that this disease affects the entire body with sickness, chills and fevers. The worst trouble is experienced when the disease moves to the lymph glands in the groin and to those that surround the anus. Bowel movements become exceedingly painful if not impossible, and the sufferer has to go to his doctor at least once a week in order to have the opening of the rectum stretched. This disease is becoming increasingly common among homosexuals because of their proclivity towards anal intercourse. Treatment is with the tetracycline drugs, but they have not as yet proved themselves absolutely curative. Indeed, some physicians say that no real or specific treatment exists as of now.

These three diseases are relatively unknown because they affect in the main only two classes of people—Negroes and homosexuals. Some very prominent people may have to come down with one or other of these illnesses before real in-depth research begins. Up to the present, it is only in the rarest instance that a white heterosexual has been stricken. This is why these three diseases are largely regarded as underground diseases. They are deceptive in their attack, almost unstoppable in their development, and devilish in their effects. Anyone who has the faintest suspicion after reading this page that he has contracted one of these diseases should drop everything and flee to the first informed doctor he can find. As is always the case, the earlier the treatment, the greater the opportunity of effecting a cure. Meantime, to all who involve themselves in any kind of promiscuity in sexual intercourse, whether it be heterosexual or homosexual, let these diseases be a warning of the dangers that lie deep within such practices. God has His own unique way of making us to reap what we sow. In these cases, the harvest is certainly awesome and terrifying.

Is there any likelihood that these diseases will spread?

There is every possible chance. If sexual promiscuity continues to develop and if homosexuality continues to rise, there is little doubt that in time all forms of VD will develop universally and astronomically. So strong is the virus and so militant are the bacteria that it is probably only a matter of time until these troubles will be known among the elite of the land. With such mutations and variables in sexual contact nowadays it seems impossible to reach any other conclusion than that we should fear and prepare for the worst. There certainly should be massive research done, and done now, on these diseases—especially lymphogranuloma venereum. There are many forms of polluting the world, and pollution is a favorite topic at the present time. This particular form of pollution should be searched out diligently and more adequate preparation made against the possibility of a major invasion.

Well, all that sounds rather bad. Are gonorrhea and syphilis not so serious?

In one sense, no. But you might as well ask, Is smallpox less serious than cancer? Neither smallpox nor cancer is desirable. They are both scourges of humanity and ravage deep into the heart of society. So with all forms of venereal disease.

Gonorrhea and syphilis are much better known than the other three, for they are far more common. They have been around for a long time, and much is known about them. But they are troubles to be feared and avoided at all costs.

Let me begin with gonorrhea. It takes at least two weeks to show up after contact has been made through sexual intercourse with someone who already has the disease. The sufferer detects a burning sensation when passing urine, and if he looks carefully, he will see that mixed with the urine is a milky white discharge. It is harder to diagnose in women than in men as it can settle in the ovaries, the womb, and the fallopian tubes. The inflammation usually lingers for some months and then fades away. This is what happens in about 95 per cent of all cases. In the remaining 5 per cent, where the trouble becomes deep-seated and stubborn, the patient may find himself unable to urinate at all, as the gonorrheal infection has gradually developed scar tissue in the urethra, which, as you may recall, is the channel that carries urine from the bladder to the outside. When complete blockage shuts off natural urination, the doctor must be called on to pass a steel rod up through the urethra to the bladder to clear the passage. Then follows the installation of a rubber catheter to drain the bladder. If the disease does not yield to treatment this form of urination by means of catheter must be pursued to life's end.

Fortunately, there is now good and effective treatment. When the sulfa drugs were introduced, it was found that they helped in overcoming the trouble. Penicillin has produced even more dramatic results. Gonorrhea became overnight a foe no longer feared. But there have been complications. In spite of the powers of penicillin and its many derivatives, gonorrhea still abounds. Indeed, as we have already noted, there has been a major rise in the incidence of syphilis and gonorrhea in recent years. This has puzzled medical observers and naturally so. Had a penicillin-resistant strain developed? It has been established that in parts of Britain certain preparations of penicillin have not been as effective as others; and recently doctors have switched to the more potent variety of medication. The fact remains, however, that the disease is still very much with us. There is no reason in the world why it could not be wiped out, but this is not happening. Why? The answer is absurdly simple. The money needed to obliterate it from the face of the earth is not being supplied by governmental agencies. This is a public health problem of the first magnitude and should be treated in the same way as we dealt with polio, typhoid, measles and the like. The situation will probably get worse before it gets better, for the spectacular rise in the number of cases in recent years augurs ill for its extermination within the near future. Perhaps some day a government will rise up that will face the facts, make the people face the facts, and demand that the whole of society be cleansed of this plague.

Is syphilis worse than gonorrhea?

You would need to define for me what you mean by worse. Both of them are dreadful diseases. Syphilis became established in Europe in about the fifteenth century and it has been with us ever since. It is a most unusual disease. As many as 50 per cent of those who contract it suffer no ill effects whatsoever. They can have the disease and yet not show any evidence of it. About a quarter of all infected people show some slight symptoms. It is the final quarter that are the real problem.

The first evidences of syphilis appear about two weeks after sexual intercourse with an infected person. This is much the same period of development as gonorrhea. A small sore appears at the location of infection—that may be on the penis or in the labia minora, but it can also appear on a fingertip, on a breast, on the lips, and in the case of homosexuals in the anus.

Quite often, the sore will disappear. The body, if it has sufficient strength to overcome the infection, prevails over it and that is all there is to it. But should it persist, and if subsequently there appear the secondary signs of skin rash, inflammation of the mouth or sexual organs, then you have a real case on your hands, and treatment should be prompt and adequate. Penicillin is absolutely the master of syphilis. This should be given in required dosage and the response will be speedy. In every case of doubt, consult a doctor. He is there to help you.

Can these diseases be transmitted to children?

They can. This is one of the saddest features about them. Syphilis can in serious cases be a crippling and debilitating disease to those adults who have it. But when you see children with inherited congenital weaknesses, you begin to see something of the immensity of the whole problem. Syphilis can be transmitted by actual inheritance to children, and they can be made to suffer from a whole range of disabling and distorted hindrances. To pass on to one's posterity such dysfunction of limbs is a very grievous act indeed. Similarly, in the case of gonorrhea a child's eyes may be affected as he passes through the vagina at birth. The answer to this has been found, and again it is absurdly simple. Newborn babies need only have their eyes treated with an application of silver nitrate solution or penicillin ointment. This should be done within moments of delivery, and if it is done there is no possibility of blindness. But there are many parts of the world where this is not known; there are many parts of the world where women do not have surgically clean hospitals to go for delivery of their babies. In areas such as these, there is still much blindness that has obviously come as the result of a gonorrheal infection. I have seen many cases of this in many different parts of the world, and especially in the Far East. It is a sobering thought that through the sin of the parent the child should be punished. God never intended that it should be so. But then God never intended that there should be promiscuity. It is in this light that we must recall—as we have had occasion to note already—that God "visits the iniquities of the parents upon the children unto the third and fourth generation." We must at the same time recall that "He shows mercy to thousands of them that love Me and keep My commandments." This is a fact that the Church must declare with unfaltering conviction. "What a man sows, he will also reap: for God is not mocked. He that sows to the flesh, shall of the flesh reap corruption; but he that soweth to the Spirit shall of the Spirit reap life everlasting" (Galatians 6:8).

Could you develop that a little more? I want to know as much as possible about the kind of suffering that the children of syphilitic parents endure.

All right. But it isn't a pleasant subject to dwell on, though there is a sense, of course, in which it is good that every evangelical Christian be fully informed about these conditions. That is another reason why this book is being written. The ignorance of the Christian public on subjects such as these is a downright disgrace. If they knew more, perhaps they would care more than they seem to do.

Babies can be infected with syphilis while in the womb. If they live, they are ruined both physically and mentally. About 25 per cent of all infected babies die before birth—a merciful release! Roughly the same number are born but die within a few weeks. For those who live on, it would be a very natural thing to say: "It would have been better if he had never been born."

Two groups of living wrecks can be distinguished. The first has a whole assortment of deformities, ranging from blindness and deafness to a distortion of leg bones and a collapse of facial bones, leaving the countenance without a nose or with an ugly and distorted mouth. The other class is not so deeply affected, but they carry with them a low-grade type of infection that can remain with them for years, during which time the tissues crack and break down, and the liver, testicles, bones and throat bear most of the punishment. There is not much that can be done for children like these. They respond well to penicillin treatment and the infection can be stopped completely. But nothing can give back sight to sightless eyes; and no drug has yet been invented that can make those hear whose ear mechanism has been permanently destroyed. If for no other reason, society should for the children's sake determine that this scourge be banished from the earth.

I find it hard to believe that God would allow such births to take place. Can you?

No, not really. A Christian man believes in the absolute sovereignty of God. To be God, He must be all-knowing, all-powerful and absolutely free. If there were one iota of knowledge that God did not possess, no matter how small it might be, His sovereignty would break down at that point. As Lord of all creation, He rules over all and He must therefore possess all knowledge. Similarly, were God lacking in one modicum of power, that lack would end His reign and destroy His kingdom. The one stray atom of knowledge would belong to someone else, and God would therefore be a limited ruler only.

At the same time, God gave man a free will. God made man in His own image. The image of God obviously encompasses processes of thought, of emotion and of volition. For man to be free, he must be really free; and that is how God made him—free not to sin, free to choose the good and to turn from the evil. Now this may be very difficult to understand; indeed, I'm sure that with the finite mind alone we cannot understand this. But one thing is easy to perceive. Only an absolutely omnipotent God could create a free being. It is only omnipotence that can create the capacity to defy omnipotence. And this God has done. In sovereignty He made man free. He gave to him the most extraordinary endowment and set him in the midst of a world that was a perfect paradise.

But man chose evil. That is the story the Bible unfolds. And out of this long and terrifying antinomy against heaven, this determined hostility of man against the God who gave him birth, there arise the kind of problems that we are discussing here. A child born blind and deformed as the result of the life his parents have lived—after all it was they who chose to have such relationships as would promote venereal disease—is a living, though distorted, example of what man's freedom really means. In his freedom he taints all he touches, he befouls all he breathes on, he blotches all his canvasses and produces monstrosities. It is indeed true that there are tremendous capacities for greatness in man. As Shakespeare exults in *Hamlet:*

> "What a piece of work is man! How noble in reason! How infinite in faculty! In form, in moving, how express and admirable! In action how like an angel! In apprehension how like a god!"

Yet, alongside of that, place these words of Sigmund Freud:

> No one who, like me, conjures up the most evil of those half-tamed demons that inhabit the human breast, and seeks to wrestle with them, can expect to come through the struggle unscathed.

Freud constantly reverts to this kind of theme. When discussing the *Anatomy of the Mental Personality,* he comments:

> One might compare the relationship of the ego to the id with that between a rider and his horse. The horse provides the locomotor energy, and the rider has the prerogative of determining the goal and of guiding the movements of his powerful mount towards it. But all too often in the relations between the ego and the id we find a picture of the less ideal situation in which the rider is obliged to guide his horse in the direction in which it itself wants to go.

At this point, we can quote Paul: "The good that I would, I do not; and the evil that I would not, that I do. O wretched man that I am, who shall deliver me from the body of this death?" (Romans 7:19, 24). Here is man's dilemma. He is made in the image of God. But he has turned to evil—and is bound. He is a slave who should be a king. And because he is sinful in disposition, he does things that are sinful in nature. God could not be God and sovereign if He had created man with anything less than a capacity to say No to good. That is what God did. And this is what man has done. And the result? The worm, the canker and the grief of blighted lives! The pain and the infinite heartache of sightless, deformed, misshapen children. This is the outcrop of sin. Let us be wise and heed the warnings that are given us.

Before we leave this whole subject, can you say whether what

you called the underground diseases are likely to break out and become more widespread?

I suppose it is right that we should speculate. At the moment, black people and homosexuals are most likely to contract one of these diseases. This may be because of something specific in the Negro race. They may have a genetic susceptibility to these venereal diseases. This is doubtful, however, as it is now clear that homosexuals also are a prey to them.

It is more likely that economic reasons are the real reasons why they are more frequently found among blacks; and that promiscuity explains their prevalence among homosexuals. The three diseases we called underground diseases are almost endemic in certain sections of the black communities. Now, if for some reason sexual intercourse between whites and blacks should begin to be more frequent—as you know, they are relatively rare in this part of the world—who can hazard a guess as to what might happen? There can be little doubt that the incidence among whites will increase; and who can say where that will end? And with the almost unbelievable growth in the homosexual population, there is very good reason to fear that the infection will be passed on in ever increasing volume. I would tend to fear the worst concerning your question.

Any final advice on the topic?

Only a word from the best of books. In Ecclesiastes 12:13-14 we read:

> Let us hear the conclusion of the matter, the whole matter: Fear God, and keep His commandments: for this is the whole duty of man. For God shall bring every work into judgment, with every secret thing, whether it be good, or whether it be evil.

I think that's a great place to leave it. "Fear God and keep His commandments."

15: Divorce

I am glad that we are to discuss divorce, even though I feel it regrettable to do so in a book on sex and marriage for Christians. First of all, what is the real situation regarding number of divorces in the Western world?

Poor. Very poor. All over the Western world the rates of divorce have been rising through most of this century. There is no other civilization of the past 1000 years that can in any way match the breakdown in marriages of men and women in the North American continent during the past generation. About one in four marriages in the U.S.A. ends in divorce. Every year about one and a half million lives—men, women and children—are upset through the breakdown of marriage.

The high-water mark in the States was reached in 1946, when so many marital situations had to be straightened out after World War II. United Nations figures show that there is no other country with a number that comes within shouting distance of the U.S. plateau. There are certainly some primitive societies where divorce is as commonplace as eating or sleeping, and there the incidence may well be higher. But in general, the rate for the rest of the Western world is about half that of the U.S.A. It is an interesting footnote, however, to these statements that *Time,* in early 1968, reported a significant upgrowth of divorce rates in several Communist-bloc countries of eastern Europe and stated bluntly that they were approximating those of the United States.

Divorce in the fullest and most formal sense is not the only gauge of marital breakdown. It is estimated that for every divorce there is another breakup or desertion. Sociologist Harold T. Christiansen states that "The United States is experiencing close to a million marital breakups each year—or about half the number of marriages that are taking place." This means that a marriage contract in the United States at the present time has about a fifty-fifty chance of remaining in being. And how much chance do those marriages have that were entered for the sake of appearance?

Do you feel that divorce has been glamorized?

Not really, though it certainly is the case that much of the publicity about divorce has involved well-known people. Does this mean that proneness to divorce is in any way linked with what men normally call success in life? On the contrary! The possibility of marriage breakdown decreases as the educational and occupational levels of the husband, or of the couple, go up. Nonetheless it is true that a kind of tinselled glamour has gathered around the idea of divorce. The press has a lot to do with this, and some journals make a specialty of such affairs. But there really is no glamour in a divorce court. When you actually get down to the hard situations in which thoughts and talk of divorce begin, you are in a world that is very far from blue skies and rainbows. In general, there is tension and bitterness in the home, the kind of bitterness that a year or two earlier would have seemed an absolute impossibility. There is bewilderment too, and usually a great sense of loneliness. Why should this be happening to me? Why should my world have fallen in like this? Very often one or both of the partners are on tranquilizers and they may look longingly at them sometimes at night and think of ending it all forever. So they sit and brood. So they lie awake and think.

I talked with Jack only last night. He showed me his divorce papers, which had just come from the county judge. They were all in order.

"Desertion?" I asked.

"Yes."

"How long were you together?"

"About nine months."

"Why did she leave you? Had you any idea at all that she was intending to leave you?"

"Oh yes, she had spoken of it for a while. She would say that things weren't at all what she had expected. She didn't like being bound to the house so much—though why she should have been I could never make out."

"Did she leave any note when she went?"

"Nothing. I came home at night and she wasn't there. The house was so quiet I could feel the stillness. Everything seemed wrong. And then suddenly I wondered if she had really gone. I called her mother. She was hard and bitter. She told me that I had got what was coming to me and that from now on I could expect to see Irene no more."

"Did you ever see her again?"

"Only once. She was with another guy, and they were talking with great animation. But she didn't see me and I moved away as fast as I could."

"Did you still love her?"

"I think so. Things hadn't been going well, you know. But out of all the girls I knew there was only one I wanted, and that was Irene. But I guess she grew tired of me; and then quit."

"Why did you decide to seek divorce?"

"Because she wanted it. She got word to me through her mother that she wanted to get married again and that she would make it easy for me. But I couldn't bear the thought of having her divorced from me over the charge of adultery. So I waited the three years till the time I could launch proceedings against her on the basis of desertion. That's why it reads as you see it."

"Glamour? No, there is no glamour in divorce. I have seen it from every angle. From the wife's, the husband's, the parents', the friends', and worst of all the children's. There is nothing but shock, bitterness, grief and a sense of death. Sometimes two will agree to separate amicably. But I haven't met up with that kind as yet. And I really doubt that such amicableness would go very deep. In all the cases of divorce in which I have had some part there has been tension and heartbreak and infinite sorrow.

What have you found to be the principal causes of divorce?

Money is one of the major reasons. Neither partner is content with the way the paycheck is divided and spent. Wrangles begin, and eventually they mushroom. Soon you imagine that your partner is deliberately saying things to annoy you. You bite your tongue and hold back what you want to say; but in another minute it comes out. You get angry, cross, irritated. Then communication breaks down. You don't talk at all. All this can come from a failure to agree on money.

Lack of pleasure in your sex life. That is another fundamental cause. Some men simply don't take the trouble to learn how to help their wives to a point where intercourse can be meaningful and happy. All they want is to use their wives' bodies to satisfy their own lusts. But this is no marriage. And any girl has a right to rebel against such tyrannical treatment. Marriage is meant for two and not only for the pleasure of one. It was ordained for the life-long help and comfort that husband and wife should give to each other both in prosperity and in adversity. But when a husband is always demanding sex from his wife and giving nothing in return, what can you expect? This is again a prime cause of divided homes and broken marriages. Most divorces happen in the first five years of marriage; the rate slackens with the passing of each succeeding five-year period. This probably means that so much of the counsel given in the early chapters of this book has not been followed. You may recall that I urged then that during the period of engagement you take every opportunity to get to know one another's eccentricities, mannerisms, habits and moods. I said that this kind of knowledge would prove invaluable in the days when you were completely alone with one another. Do you remember? Then I added that one of the great reasons why God gave sexual intercourse was to cement the marriage bond and to tie husband and wife more closely than would otherwise be possible. That is absolutely basic teaching. And when it is neglected, when either the husband or the wife denies the other the God-given capacity he or she possesses, then it is very easy for love to grow cold. A truly satisfying sex-life will keep a husband and wife together through almost anything; and it gets more wonderful as the years go by.

I talked with Sally about this.

"There's just no point in my trying again. Jim has proved to be the most selfish person I've ever met. I didn't realize it before. When we were engaged everything seemed all right. But I tell you it takes a bed to let you know what a man is really like. He would come into bed some nights after never a word all evening and then he would begin to say some of the things that he used to say before we were married; and I would begin to think: 'Well, maybe he is really changing.' But no sir! All he wanted was to use me; and after he had got what he wanted he would turn his back on me and fall asleep. You can take that only so long. I've taken it for four years; and that's already too many."

She left Jim. Eventually he sued her for divorce on the ground of her desertion. But if I am certain of anything, it is that Sally was not the cause of the break in that home. Jim was. He was treating his wife as a thing and not as a person, and that is one of the quickest ways to destroy any true interpersonal relationships. I couldn't blame Sally. All my sympathies were with her. And it brought home to me once more something that I have noted over and over again—that it is often difficult to say who the real culprit is in cases of desertion. A wife may leave, but she may have had to do so to preserve her sanity. This I have seen, and my heart has wept as I have listened to the bitter cries of some broken-hearted and almost demented girl whom I had married with the brightest hopes that everything before her was lovely and beautiful and fair. Robert Haas has said that "if men would give to their married life one-tenth of the trouble and thought they give to their business, the majority of marriages would be happy." How true! You draw dividends only on what you invest.

What other legal grounds are there for which divorce may be granted?

Adultery is ground for a divorce in every state of the U.S.A. It is the same in Canada and many other countries. Other grounds are pregnancy at marriage by another man and unbeknown to the husband; impotence; sexual malformation; non-support; mental cruelty; physical cruelty; habitual drunkenness; habitual use of drugs; venereal disease; mental incapacity; post-marital insanity; conviction of a felony; life imprisonment; refusal to co-habit. These grounds vary from state to state in the Union. Sterility, for instance, is grounds for divorce in only two states—Mississippi (if undisclosed at time of marriage) and Utah (if existing at the inception of marriage). In Connecticut, sexual malformation making intercourse impossible is grounds for divorce under terms of fraudulent contract. Other grounds for divorce in different parts of the country are sodomy, and buggery—meaning sexual intercourse of men with animals; instances where either party to the marriage had been guilty of a heinous offense and did not declare this to the other partner in the marriage prior to the wedding; and in some places, instances in which the wife was a prostitute before marriage.

Must one of the parties always be proved through the courts to be the responsible or guilty party?

Yes. That is the way in which things are done in our part of the world. Most state laws demand that to sue for divorce an adversary proceeding must be adopted; that is, one of the parties must be proven by the other to be guilty of indecent, immoral, cruel or inhuman behavior. Evidence for this must be gathered—unless, of course, one party agrees not to contest the issue and to plead guilty right away. The result of this is that most partings through divorce are made only after the wounds have been made very deep. This is a matter for deep regret, though it is difficult to see how else the case can proceed. An interesting and very sad statistic is that children of divorcees are nearly twice as likely to undergo divorce themselves as the average newlywed.

Have you any idea how much extra-marital intercourse there is in our society?

The Kinsey Reports of 1948 and 1953 supply evidence that by the age of forty, about 50 per cent of all husbands, and about 25 per cent of all wives have engaged at least once in extra-marital coitus. A further analysis of about 1100 married women who volunteered evidence to the Kinsey researchers indicated that about 16 per cent of all these women had engaged in extra-marital petting but had not gone all the way to full intercourse. Of the 25 per cent of women who had engaged in extra-marital coitus, two-fifths of them had done so in the first year of their marriage. There have been some studies more recent than the Kinsey Reports, though not quite so far-reaching in their scope. The Family Service Association of America, for instance, had responses from 154 of their agencies on the post-1960 development of infidelity in the United States. Two-thirds of the groups reporting stated that infidelity had become still more common than during the previous ten years; and many of them felt that the situation was going to grow worse in the future. If we may refer back again to Kinsey, he states that women are most likely to be unfaithful in their late thirties, whereas the probability of a husband's being unfaithful decreases from his twenties onwards.

What are the reasons given for this growth?

Many! The general permissive atmosphere of our society, with its constant overtones of sensuality, provide married people with an implied license to try out their powers of attraction on others than their own life-partner. The improved contraceptive techniques have, of course, made all illicit love affairs much less dangerous. Furthermore, with advancing years there is often a deeply sensed need in a man to overcome feelings of sexual inadequacy; and how better than by conquering another woman? Similarly, as a woman grows older she may want reassurance that she is still attractive and desirable. There are of course those cases where either partner is looking for a substitute to shore up a brittle marriage. There are also the feelings that rise within a woman whose husband has to travel a great deal in connection with his business while she is left either alone or with the children to tend. Such feelings can become very tense and overpowering. All that is needed is for the right kind of man to come along at the moment when the wife is feeling particularly unhappy, and she is an all too willing victim or conniver in an affair. Added to all these, we must note the high increase in the consumption of alcohol. Cocktail parties are good spots for letting your guard down just a little; conscience is easily mastered by a few drinks, and very soon another dupe is sacrificed on the altar of liquor.

Is there any pattern in the type of people who indulge in extramarital coitus?

Not really. They are to be found in all sorts of society, in every social level, and in every financial grouping. Rich and poor alike have lately been drawn into the maelstrom of action from which divorce can readily flow. A novel and incongruous twist has been given to the whole debate in recent times by the practice known as wife-swapping. It is not an isolated phenomenon. It is appearing in the most unlikely places and has become an occasional topic of study at conferences on the family and home. I only mention it at this point to indicate another trend downwards towards the abyss of moral decay in society. All one can say about the types of people who indulge in extra-marital affairs is that they don't have very long memories, for in the marriage ceremony they promised to keep themselves faithful for each other alone. They are also weak in the realm of conscience. But perhaps that is an inevitable factor in the sexual wilderness in which we live today. Women of active mind and balanced personality, who at the same time remain essentially feminine but hold fast to an enlightened conscience, are really very rare. To be such a person they must understand their own nature, their weaknesses and their powers. They must understand also their husband's weaknesses and follies and be generous in regarding them. When they are confident of their husband's devotion, there is seldom great cause for fear that they will prove unfaithful. As Goethe says:

> The woman whose husband is steadfast and full of good grace,
> Shows forth his troth and love, in her happy face.

And Th. H. Van De Velde in his book *Ideal Marriage* adds this:

> Behold what love can do!
> Cripples it maketh hale,
> Brings peace the world into,
> Hushes the slanderous tale;
> Fills up the home with joy,
> And tranquil blessedness.
> And though the world annoy,
> Love's name is steadfastness.

True youth lasts so long as we are loved. Any break in the marriage must lead back to some breakdown of love. A marriage is really a mockery where there is no love. It has been well said that true love does not count the years. Why should it? That is what the writer of the Book of Proverbs meant, I think, when he said:

> Better is little with the fear of the Lord than great treasure and trouble therewith.

> Better is a dinner of herbs where love is, than a stalled ox and hatred therewith (Proverbs 15:16, 17).

By deft Hebrew parallelism he equates "the fear of the Lord" with "love." That is the truly biblical view, and it is the only view that true Christians can hold. The greater the man's soul, the greater he loves. And when the love of God in all its unknowable length and breadth and height fills any man, his love will be constant, strong, considerate and selfless.

Nothing has as yet been said about the Christian attitude to divorce. Can you give some guidance on this?

Well, I'll try. There is some Mosaic legislation that should be studied carefully; there are some passages in which the teaching of Christ is summarized; and there are also a few very specific remarks by St. Paul.

Under the Mosaic law, divorce was permitted, tolerated and practiced. The passage is Deuteronomy 24:1-4, which is a crucial passage for our understanding of the Hebrew practice and the reasons for it. Here is how it reads in the New English Bible:

> When a man has married a wife, but she does not win his favour because of something shameful in her, and he writes her a note of divorce, gives it to her, and dismisses her:
>
> And suppose after leaving his house she goes off to be the wife of some other man,
>
> And this next husband turns against her and writes her a note of divorce which he gives her and dismisses her, or dies after making her his wife—
>
> Then, in that case her first husband who dismissed her is not free to take her back to be his wife again after she has become for him unclean. This is abominable to the Lord; you must not bring sin upon the land which the Lord your God is giving you as your patrimony.

The reference to "something shameful" in the first line clearly involves some kind of gross abnormality. Practices had arisen which had gone far to annul the primal law of marriage and this law is here given to restrain these as far as possible. Divorce was *suffered* under the law of Moses but it is not at all clear that it was *sanctioned.* It was "for the hardness of men's hearts" that this ordinance was passed, and with a view to slowing the rate of marital breakdown. This is as far as I think we can go in regards to the Old Testament position. For fuller understanding we must study this same passage in the light of the teaching of Christ and of St. Paul.

Can you list or read for us the various passages?

Certainly. Here they are. Let's write them fully into the record.

> *Matthew 5:31-32:*
>
> "It also used to be said that whoever divorces his wife must give her a proper certificate of divorce. But I say to you that whoever divorces his wife except on the ground of unfaithfulness is making her an adulteress. And whoever marries the woman who has been divorced also commits adultery."
>
> *Matthew 19:3-8:*
>
> Then the Pharisees arrived with a test question. "Is it right," they asked, "for a man to divorce his wife on any grounds whatsoever?"
>
> "Haven't you read," He answered, "that the One who created them from the beginning made them male and female and said: 'For this cause shall a man leave his father and mother, and shall cleave to his wife; and the twain shall become one flesh'? So they are no longer two separate people but one. No man therefore must separate what God has joined together."
>
> "Then why," they retorted, "did Moses command us to give a written divorce-notice and dismiss the woman?"
>
> "It was because you knew so little of the meaning of love that Moses allowed you to divorce your wives. But that was not the original principle."

Matthew 19:9:

"I tell you that anyone who divorces his wife on any grounds except her unfaithfulness and marries some other woman commits adultery."

Mark 10:2-12:

Then some Pharisees arrived with this test question. "Is it right for a man to divorce his wife?"

Jesus replied by asking them, "What has Moses commanded you to do?"

"Moses allowed us to write a divorce-notice and then to dismiss her," they said.

"Moses gave you that commandment," returned Jesus, "because you knew so little of the meaning of love. But from the beginning of the creation, God made them male and female. 'For this cause shall a man leave his father and mother, and shall cleave to his wife; and the twain shall become one flesh.' So that in body they are no longer two people but one. That is why man must never separate what God has joined together."

On reaching the house, his disciples asked him again about this matter.

"Any man who divorces his wife and marries another woman," He told them, "commits adultery against his wife. And if she divorces her husband and marries someone else, she commits adultery."

Luke 16:18:

"Any man who divorces his wife and marries another woman commits adultery. And so does any man who marries the woman who was divorced from her husband."

Is it not the case that in these we have divergent accounts of Christ's teaching about divorce?

No! I do not think so. When you study these passages carefully, you will see that in Matthew 5:32 and 19:9 there is the absolutely important qualification "except for unfaithfulness." When this happens, the marriage is dissolved in the sight of God immediately. Anything else that can follow will only be a formalization of what God has ordained. Adultery is listed as a prime cause here for divorce. There is no question as to the accuracy of the text; and there is no point in our getting involved in exegetical gymnastics when we are dealing with the basic teaching of the New Testament. As I read the New Testament, I see here that Christ states very categorically that adultery destroys the marriage bond. I believe also that implicit at the heart of all His teaching, the rights of the woman are cared for as well as the rights of the man. Great arguments have raged around these passages: Which of them is prior and therefore more authentic? How does it happen that neither Mark nor Luke refers to the exception that is so clearly stated in Matthew 5:32 and 19:9? And so on. But I take it that when the teaching of Christ is set alongside that of St. Paul, as contained particularly in I Corinthians 7:10-15 and Romans 7:1-3, there can be no doubt that divorce is allowable on the ground of adultery, and that remarriage after such a breakdown is sanctioned by God. There is no conflict between Christ and Paul. Paul pleads with the Corinthians to observe the claims of honor, purity and piety that the marriage bond has laid upon them. He states that husband and wife are one flesh, and that neither should leave the other. He does say that "if for some particular reason the wife depart from her husband, let her remain unmarried" (I Corinthians 7:10). In this he is stressing the indissolubility of the marriage tie and is expressly warning against possible adultery. Paul and our Lord are at one in their emphasis. Marriage is for life. It is intended by God that husband and wife should live together until death. Anything else is sub-Christian.

But Romans 7:1-3 makes it still clearer that Paul recognizes that adultery cancels out the bond of marriage. "If, while her husband liveth, she be married to another man, she shall be called an adulteress." The teaching is identical with that of Matthew 5:32 and 19:9, and from all this I deduce that the standards of the Bible are uniform, absolute and categorical. Marriage is for life. This is God's intent. It can be broken only by adultery. Where that has occurred, the marriage is already dissolved in the sight of God.

You are suggesting then that there are no other grounds on which a Christian might seek divorce?

Yes. That is what I am saying.

I am well aware of all the compelling reasons for lowering the standard in our day. I know only too well what agony can be imposed where adultery is the sole basis for dissolving of a marriage. I know also how frequently evidence is forged or freely made available in order to secure a dissolution of marriage by court order. But the mere breakdown of a marriage is no valid ground for divorce. Dire sickness—prolonged mental illness for example—is no valid ground for divorce. In a materialistically minded society and in a very secular world such as ours has become, it may be very easy to bring forward grounds on which marriage should be dissolved more easily and without bitterness if possible. But that is not what we are studying at the moment. Our question is this: What is the Christian rule regarding divorce? And to that question I see only one answer: Marriage is dissolved only by adultery or death.

Why should the state have such interest in cases of divorce?

This is quite a long story, but an interesting one. In England, divorce was originally under the jurisdiction of the ecclesiastical courts, and these courts followed what were known as the Canon Laws. These courts could grant a divorce from bed and board—a kind of partial divorce more like separation—and they also could rule on the original validity of the marriage. But they were not permitted to give a total divorce from the bond of marriage. This power was jealously guarded by Parliament. In 1857, by act of Parliament, judicial courts were established with powers to rule on the validity of the original marriage and also with powers to grant complete dissolution of the marriage.

This state of affairs never existed in the United States, for matrimonial law was never accepted as part of the common law. Suits for divorce must be brought under legal statute only; and in the intricate structure of our federal system, it is the state and not the federal government which legislates on divorce. Each state has its own grounds for divorce. The reason why the state has such an interest in the question of divorce—and only now am I really getting to the point of answering your question—is that marriage is a legal relation of a particular nature with certain mutual rights and obligations, and these obligations are determined not by common consent among two parties but by the general law. The state has an interest in every marriage. The state knows that the family unit is the true and best arena for the training of its citizens. It is therefore very concerned to ensure that marriage is not regarded lightly or that it can be terminated at the mere whim of the people concerned. The relation can be dissolved only for what the state considers to be good and valid grounds; and these grounds are established by the legislature and become law. Decrees of divorce are valid only within the area of jurisdiction in which the decree is granted, and so the domicile or place of residence of the parties becomes all-important too. I know a man divorced in Montana who is now a resident in Canada and has remarried, but Canada does not recognize the original divorce. A bit complicated, isn't it?

It sure is. What about property rights, custody of children and such matters; does the court rule on these also?

Yes! By the divorce decree, the custody of the children, if there are children, is usually given, at the discretion of the court, to one of the parties, the best welfare of the children being the principal consideration. On certain grounds, the wife may be entitled to alimony, and this too is set by the court. She may retain her husband's name if she so desires. Both parties are usually free to remarry although this is not an invariable rule. Sometimes a time-limit within which neither of the parties may remarry is imposed. This, sad to say, has really very little effect, as most parties who are under such stricture just settle in and live in a common-law relationship until the date when they can marry again.

What have you found to be the greatest problem associated with divorce?

The children, of course! They are the greatest sufferers in every way. They are still young and unable to understand why their parents have disagreed, though they realize only too well when tension fills the home. How well a child can determine the climate of the home for the day by a look at either his father's or his mother's face! But when the climax comes and custody of the children is given to one parent with possible visiting rights to the other at stated times, the child finds himself in a most difficult position.

How can you explain divorce to a child? To a young child you may say: "Your Mummy and Daddy fight too much, just as you and Chester Franklin used to fight. We have decided that rather than keep on fighting, it is better for us to live in different homes; but Daddy will still be your Daddy, and Mummy will still be your Mummy." Tragic, is it not? But millions of children have had to be told something like that. The care of the children of divorcees should be one of the greatest concerns of the Church of Christ. We have much to give them. And they are so eager to take what we give.

Sometimes one of the parents simply disappears. How do you explain this to the children?

It is very difficult to compensate for an irreparable loss. But time is a greater healer and, if the job is handled well, there is no reason why the child should not become well adjusted to life. Chuck Jones is a good example. I talked with him recently.

"I remember," he said, "the first day it dawned on me that Dad had really left us. We all knew that Mum and he had been having disagreements and sometimes quite violent quarrels, but we never thought it would come to this. Then one day Mum told all of us kids that a divorce had been given them and that from then on we would be under her care, though Dad could see us quite often. I was stunned. I hated him. I never wanted to see him again. I told Mum so; but she said I was wrong so I quit saying it. Then after six months had gone by and Dad never showed up, I began to wish I'd never said what I'd said, and began to wish to see him again. But he never came. He never came back. He just lit out and left us cold. I guess the alimony he had to meet got him down and he decided he'd be better out of our life completely. Mum has done her best. I think we've all helped. I got a paper route and kept it for four years until I got something else with more money. But I sometimes still find myself wanting to see him and to be able to say: 'That's my Dad.' You know, the hardest thing was trying to explain to the other kids at school what had happened. We all lied about it. We said he was overseas in some job and was making big money. But somehow they knew. I guess they heard from their homes what the real thing was."

What the real thing was. Yes! In the wake of divorce, there is nothing but sorrow, grief, mortification, anger and despair. God never planned it so.

16: Sex and Marriage and God

Well, I guess we've covered most of the questions that were in our minds. But I'm sure you still have some things that you want to say.

Not very much. There is certainly a vast difference between the biblical concept of marriage and the prevailing worldly view. The normal view of the non-Christian is that marriage is a convenient relationship whereby you observe the expectations of the society in which you have been reared and in which you also have an orderly and convenient way to enjoy sex. Sexuality on a biblical view is a fundamental part of being human. The capacity for sex is built into the very essence of your personality. Sex is different from eating or drinking. You can eat and drink and not really involve yourself. But sex is different. Sexuality affects your total person. Your essential selfhood is affected by it. But even so, the biblical view of marriage is never built on sex. It has far stronger and more abiding foundations, for it is built and grounded in the sovereign act of God's creation. All true marriage is a creative act of God.

This is getting just a little beyond me. Can you make it more simple.

I'll try. Marriage appears in the very earliest pages of the Bible. It is, if I may put it this way, built into the creative ordinance of God. In the biblical accounts which we have in Genesis, it is God who brings Eve to Adam. Similarly, in our modern Christian marriage ceremony, usually the father of the bride leads her to the altar and "gives her away" to the bridegroom. In this, we are fulfilling the symbolism of Genesis and affirming that in this act of marriage we are going right back to the first records and following them in word and deed, thus indicating that we believe it is God who has brought these two together. It is for the same reason that Jesus said that "what God has joined together, let not man put asunder" (Matthew 19:6). Marriage is thus far more than a social contract or convention. It is an act of God. God is at work in it, making man and woman one flesh and in and by them creating new life.

Rising from this is another fact, equally fundamental. It is that the biblical foundation for monogamy is the fact that God's basic unit of creation is not one individual human being, male or female, but Man and Woman as one reality, one flesh. It is the unity of man and woman that is made in the image of God, not man without woman, or woman without man. It is when a man and woman come together with this full understanding of the mind and will of God that they really participate actively in the sovereign will of God. In their union they reflect the image of God. God's creative act is constantly being completed whenever marriage takes place between a man and woman. This being so, since they are truly one through God's creative act, and since they reflect the very oneness of God in the oneness of their marriage, it is altogether unthinkable that they should ever separate. This is why adultery is viewed, both in the Old and New Testaments, as so serious a sin. It is not only a breakup of a most solemn compact; it is an attack on the very image of God Himself. It is an assault against the being of God and the highest of His creation, namely man and woman, one flesh. It is impossible to exaggerate this. The biblical record is so clear and should constantly be before the eyes of every bride and groom. "So God created man in His own image, in the image of God created He him; male and female He created them" (Genesis 1:27). Do you see how there is this significant movement from "him" to "them"? This is the foundation of the biblical doctrine of marriage. It is a holy state of life, for in it you are sharing and participating in the life of God—Father, Son and Holy Spirit.

This makes marriage, then, one of life's supreme acts?

Of course it does. And to say anything less than this is to play around with the truth. Marriage is God's act. It is He who "joins together." For anyone to break the unity that God has effected in marriage and to have an adulterous union with another outside of marriage is to force God to share in the adultery—which is a very terrible thing to contemplate. The New Testament teaching is crystal clear; and we assume that the Old Testament intent is fulfilled in the revelation of the New Testament. Man and woman are joined together by an act of God—"in the Lord." Thus, their marriage affects their relationships not only with one another and with society but also with the Lord. Sexual acts outside of the holy bond of matrimony are acts against the Name of the Lord and will be judged as such. The result of all this is that when for fun or experimentation a man and woman engage in pre-marital or extra-marital acts of sexual intercourse, they are playing fast and loose with God and prostituting the holy creative act of God to their own selfish ends.

We come back at this point to what I said in the very beginning of this book. God has His own choice for you. Every man's life has a divine blueprint written in heaven. God knows the one with whom you should be joined together. In the wonder of His providence He will cause you to meet, to fall in love, and then graciously fulfill what is basic in the very heart of creation, to be joined as one in the bond of wedlock. In this you fulfill the will of God. But to anticipate God, to try by trial and error to discover what sex is like and to have illicit unions with another, to refuse to await the day of His appointment when He will give you the one of His choosing, all this is a repudiation of the basic union which God has made to exist between man and woman. Let God bring your bride to your side. Wait till God brings that husband to your side. You will never regret it.

What you are saying is that God's ethic is unalterable?

Yes! That's what I'm saying. There is no alteration in the divine program for man; the basic unit of creation is Man-Woman in a God-given unity. And anyone sharing in marriage recognizes that this is an act of God. The ceremony of marriage becomes an actual participation in God's act. Otherwise, you are left with everything relative. Sex and marriage become matters of social custom or psychological convenience and nothing more. There is nothing of an absolute about them. They have only the sanction of social custom or financial gain or pragmatic convenience.

This becomes really serious when you follow through the implications to their logical conclusion. This is what Dr. Robinson did when he was Bishop of Woolwich and wrote his book *Honest to God.* He averred that the basic image of God was changeable, that there is no unalterable image of Jesus, and that therefore Christian ethics can be changed, can become the ethic of the moment or of the occasion. Situational ethics are the real core of Christianity. As a result of this, Dr. Robinson had little difficulty with such books as *Lady Chatterley's Lover* by D. H. Lawrence. What you find in the covers of that book is a natural form of evolution or change, of alteration and mutation, from the absolute rigidity of an unchangeable ethic. But God in fact doesn't change. To say that God is immutable is to say that He never differs from Himself. There is no concept of a growing or of a developing God in the Scriptures. For a moral person to change, he must do so in one of three possible directions: from better to worse, from worse to better, or from one order of being to another. But it is impossible to think of God in this way. No deterioration within the unspeakably holy nature of God is conceivable. No mutation of the divine essence is possible. God is God. That is the end of the matter. He changes not. So Frederick Faber sings:

O Lord! my heart is sick,
Sick of this everlasting change;
And life runs tediously quick
Through its unresting race and varied range:
Change finds no likeness to itself in Thee,
And wakes no echo in Thy mute Eternity.

God is absolute. His ethic is absolute and unchanging. What was ordained in life's primal dawning is still binding on all mankind forever and forever.

Fidelity to one another is, then, the supreme virtue in marriage?

Exactly. Fidelity to one another is clearly interwined with true love and cannot be separated from such love in a properly fulfilled union. Love in its first and fullest vigor pledges itself to a total fidelity; and the continual observance of this leads on to an ever deepening and maturing love. There is no kind of domination intended in this. On the contrary, true love is gentle and considerate, compassionate and kind. In *Sex and Sanity* (1965), Stuart Babbage comments on this:

> Lordship within marriage means not aggressive domination, but humble service. It means eager and solicitous concern for the happiness and welfare of the other. The wife, for her part, is to respond to her husband's loving concern with cheerful obedience.

The fidelity of which we speak is exemplified best of all in the fidelity with which Christ loves His Church. It was for her that He gave Himself on the Cross. It was because of His great love that He stooped so low in order to win her from sin. And His love never ends. Changeless as the everlasting hills, His love remains the same. He is constant and unwavering in His love for His Church. And the marriage bond, as we have already seen and as St. Paul so clearly emphasizes, is the human and earthly symbol of the relationship between Christ and His Church. There is a heavenly prospect for the people of God that sees them joined forever with Him, the Head and Saviour of His body and bride, the Church. God's fidelity never breaks or bends. Neither should the fidelity of husband and wife for one another.

Emil Brunner speaking of marriage in *The Divine Imperative* adds emphasis from another direction.

> It is a mistake to say: "If the love is genuine, it will be permanent!" That is simply bad psychology. Of course love, as a fact of nature, means, "intends," to last forever, but it cannot guarantee its permanence. . . . The spiritual, personal sense of being bound causes natural love, which is itself unstable, to become stable; it is this, and not the rare exception of a naturally permanent inexhaustible energy of love, which is the secret of a "happy" marriage.

And Luther in his *Table Talk* adds this: "There is no more lovely, friendly and charming relationship, communion or company than a good marriage." When two people really love one another, there is nothing more imperative, nothing more delightful, than *giving:*

giving always and everything—one's thoughts, one's life, one's body, and all that one has. This is true fidelity. Here is the unchangeableness that an unchanging God by the Holy Spirit can make us to know. True marriage is total community of purpose, of experience, of activity, of plans and dreams, of hopes and visions. There is something lacking if marriage for you has not yet reached that stage.

From what you are saying I see that Christian marriage is really a proclamation of the Gospel.

How right you are! And how glad I am that this is the note that has come through in what I've been saying. The Good News is proclaimed by life as well as by lip, and since that is so, where can there be a better place for demonstrating the heart of the Good News than at the heart of a true marriage and a gracious, Christian home? True love and true marriage will always cut right through self-centeredness and selfishness, which are the root of unbelief, and they will open up the glorious horizons of life and love that stream with brilliant intensity from the pages of God's Book.

When the Apostle Peter speaks to husbands and wives and reminds them that they are "heirs together of the grace of life," he repeats himself a bit, but only to make his meaning clearer. "Similarly you husbands should try to understand the wives you live with, honouring them as physically weaker yet equally heirs with you of the grace of life. If you don't do this, you will find it impossible to pray properly" (I Peter 3:7). Effective prayer, the kind of prayer that God answers, is linked here with the strength of Christian affection at home. Similarly, where the love of God is shed abroad in a truly Christian marriage, there His Word is being made known. Witness is being made to the beauty of the Christian virtues and graces and to Christ who is the Head of the home. The world on every hand desperately needs to see this kind of witness. It is high time that Christians stopped making their homes a mere sham of religious pretense. Our homes are intended by God to reflect His glory; and when they do, then the love of Christ comes blazing through. Christian marriage can prove one of the most effective means of witnessing to the salvation we have found in Christ. Where that love is lacking, something is wrong. If it is lacking, look and find the reason; then get busy and work out your problems.

Properly understood, a marriage that is truly Christian, taking place within the framework of the Body of Christ, the Church, the Body of the Reconciled, is an act which proclaims the love of God, preaches the reconciling grace of Christ, and bears witness of the re-creation of the human race in one family of God. In all truly Christian marriages, divisions are healed and the sins of separatism and divisiveness are forgiven and cleansed. Marriage thus becomes for the Christian one of the greatest ways to let men know the wonder of

> The love that drew salvation's plan,
> The grace that brought it down to man,
> And the mighty gulf that God did span
> At Calvary.

It is into this kind of marriage that we are called. "They who will learn love will always be its scholars." I read this once and don't know where I read it. But it certainly stresses what we have been saying all the way through. Let love reign, and go on to know more and more of the love of God which passes knowledge. Then will your love be like a beacon to others in the dark pointing them on to the way that is everlasting and the life that is filled with all the fulness of God.

What you say reminds me that it was at a wedding that Christ performed His first miracle.

It happened in Cana of Galilee. What a day that must have been! We know nothing of the couple who were being wed. Isn't it strange how silent the Bible sometimes can be about things we would long to know? What we do know is that Jesus and His disciples were invited. Mary, mother of Jesus, was also there. Then, when everything seemed to be set for a wonderful time, disaster struck. There was no wine. Shame filled the hearts of those who were responsible for the entertaining of the guests. They had failed them; and they couldn't understand how it had happened.

But Jesus was there. And where Jesus is, there is joy. His mother said to the servants, "Be sure and do everything that He tells you to do." Strange orders were given. They had to take the water jars that were actually used for the Jewish ceremonial cleansing, and they were to fill them to the brim. Then Jesus said, "Take this to the master of ceremonies." That was all. He spoke; and it was done. He gave the simplest of orders; and the water turned to wine. Without fanfare or shouting or the beating of any drums, the miracle happened. It happened because Jesus Christ was there. That was a truly Christ-filled wedding; and since that day, the story has been told again and again of how the Lord of Joy turned the waters of earth into the brimming wine of heaven. He is still doing it. I could take you to hundreds of homes in this lovely city of Toronto and show you the difference that Christ makes. He is Lord of all beauty, of all pleasure, of all melody and dancing. He is Lord over all.

Wherever He is, the best is being bettered. That's what the master of ceremonies found. "You have kept the best wine until now." With Christ, the end is always better than the beginning. With Him, the best is always yet to be. Make sure, then, that whatever else you do when you come to the moment of being joined in holy wedlock, you make certain that Jesus the Christ is there. Nothing will perfect the day but His presence. Let Him be the first invited guest. Let Him work the miracle of His love at your wedding. And out of the joy of your wedding may there be many who will come to believe in Him as Saviour, Lord and Friend.

Any final word?

At many weddings I have read J. B. Phillips' translation of First Corinthians, chapter 13. For me, it is surpassingly beautiful. Let me end with it—with telling again the marks of the love of God that purifies and perfects all our loves.

> If I speak with the eloquence of men and of angels, but have no love, I become no more than blaring brass or crashing cymbal. If I have the gift of foretelling the future and hold in my mind not only all human knowledge but the very secrets of God, and if I also have that absolute faith which can move mountains, but have no love, I amount to nothing at all. If I dispose of all that I possess, yes, even if I

give my own body to be burned, but have no love, I achieve precisely nothing.

This love of which I speak is slow to lose patience—it looks for a way of being constructive. It is not possessive: it is neither anxious to impress nor does it cherish inflated ideas of its own importance.

Love has good manners and does not pursue selfish advantage. It is not touchy. It does not keep account of evil or gloat over the wickedness of other people. On the contrary, it is glad with all good men when truth prevails.

Love knows no limit to its endurance, no end to its trust, no fading of its hope; it can outlast anything. It is, in fact, the one thing that still stands when all else has fallen.

For if there are prophecies they will be fulfilled and done with, if there are "tongues" the need for them will disappear, if there is knowledge it will be swallowed up in truth. For our knowledge is always incomplete and our prophecy is always incomplete, and when the complete comes, that is the end of the incomplete.

When I was a little child I talked and felt and thought like a little child. Now that I am a man my childish speech and feeling and thought have no further significance for me.

At present we are men looking at puzzling reflections in a mirror. The time will come when we shall see reality whole and face to face! At present all I know is a little fraction of the truth, but the time will come when I shall know it as fully as God now knows me!

In this life we have three great lasting qualities—faith, hope and love. But the greatest of them is love.

Where hearts are opened to the inflow of God's mighty ocean of everlasting love, His miracles are known. The day of miracles is very much with us. I pray that your wedding day and the years of your marriage will prove this true.

Index of Subjects

Index of Biblical References